Getting It Done

Building a future without bankrupting the present

The Story of the New Niagara Falls High School

By

Mike Kurilovitch

© 2003 by Mike Kurilovitch. All rights reserved.

No part of this book may be reproduced, stored in a retrieval system, or transmitted by any means, electronic, mechanical, photocopying, recording, or otherwise, without written permission from the author.

ISBN: 1-4107-2264-3 (e-book)
ISBN: 1-4107-2265-1 (Paperback)

Library of Congress Control Number: 2003090969

This book is printed on acid free paper.

Printed in the United States of America
Bloomington, IN

1stBooks - rev. 04/22/03

Foreword

Dr. Lawrence Lezotte

Individuals and communities need stability to survive, but change is equally important. To survive, and to thrive, we all need a balance of stability and change, in our lives and in our world. We need to harness these opposing forces to work in concord. It can be done; it was done in Niagara Falls.

The new Niagara Falls (New York) High School now symbolizes the union of stability and change for the hundreds of individuals whose lives were touched by this facility. The entire Niagara Falls community was affected, and the staff and students of both (the former) LaSalle and Niagara Falls high schools will never be the same again. Only time will tell how much impact the opportunities created at the new school will have, on its students and on the city itself.

The "new" Niagara Falls High School, main entrance. This twilight photograph taken before installation of the illuminated clock tower

The story of the new Niagara Falls High School is actually hundreds of stories, each from a different perspective. It is a story of a community coming to terms with change, politically and economically, using new and innovative ways of funding school construction. It is a story of bricks and mortar, incorporating many unique architectural features never before seen in schools. It is a story of educational change, incorporating state of the art technology, the latest educational research, and the best of past educational practice. It is a story of the building of new relationships among faculty, students, and different segments of the community. It is a story of personal change involving hundreds of teachers, school administrators, board members, and literally thousands of students. Finally, and perhaps most significantly, it is a story of hope and renewal.

It would be impossible for one book to convey how each individual and every community group was influenced by the new high school. This book captures enough of their stories to enable the reader to appreciate how individual lives, and an entire city, changed forever. In doing so, the book weaves a rich tapestry for those who did not experience this transformation first hand.

We've all heard the old expression that says, for want of a nail the horseshoe was lost, leading to the loss of the horse, the rider, and ultimately the war itself. I believe the reverse is also true. Provide the nail and the shoe is saved, thus saving the horse, the rider, and ultimately winning the war. The new Niagara Falls High School may well serve as the nail, and as the symbol of a new beginning for this proud city and school district.

In the future, I believe Niagara Falls, New York will be recognized for more than its famous falls. Niagara Falls will also be recognized by educational and civic leaders everywhere for its vision, courage, leadership, and collaboration symbolized by its new Niagara Falls High School.

INTRODUCTION

Niagara Falls, New York.

The "Magic Dateline," to those in the media. The "Honeymoon Capital of the World," to everyone on the sunny side of, say, 80 degrees west longitude.

But to many of the 55,000 or so hardy souls remaining here — and the number seems to plunge daily, like so much water churning over that acclaimed precipice — the world's former "Power City" is something else entirely:

Naysayer Capital of the Universe.

For all practical intents and purposes, "NIMBY" — that fashionable environmental catch phrase of the 80s and 90s — may have originated right here. The words "Not In My Back Yard" seem to spout from every affected corner when ever a project or development is proposed, regardless of its nature and regardless of its potentially positive impact.

An expansive theme venture to resurrect a forgotten Main Street? NIMBY.

A downtown mega-mall that would be the envy of all? Maybe, but NIMBY.

A state-of-the-art high school that would double as a sort of community square, unifying the city while hosting untold scores of events? Sounds great — as long as it's NIMBY.

Oh, and don't plan on using my tax dollars for it, either.

A sad state of affairs, indeed, for a once-proud, internationally acclaimed city.

But who can blame skeptical Niagarans? After all, defeatist attitudes come naturally after experiencing decades of downtown decay, neatly packaged and sold to the masses as "urban renewal."

Pessimism becomes a euphemism in the face of atrocities like the Love Canal environmental disaster.

And mistrust runs rampant in the presence of mismanagement, a familiar face to generations of Niagarans. Hordes of self-serving leaders practicing partisan politics and patronage have presided over the city's protracted decline, seemingly helpless to halt the hemorrhage of jobs and people.

Like a plague it has been, in terms of devastation. And the survivors, understandably, have become hardened. Obstructionism and negativity, on the part of residents and leaders alike, have manifested as just a couple of the many legitimate — albeit deleterious — side effects.

That was then, and that is now.

And thus it was, back in 1996, when the Niagara Falls City School District first proposed closing its two existing buildings and merging the city's nearly 2,500 high school students in a new, state-of-the-art facility. An educational edifice that would be the envy of virtually every teenager, not to mention every educator of teens, both here and abroad.

Oh, the couch critics had a veritable field day with that one. Too many kids in one place! You won't be able to manage it! Just asking for trouble, they said. Ever hear of Columbine?

The dreaded NIMBY, of course, rose like a collective war cry from every conceivable nook and cranny.

A world-class school on picture-postcard property overlooking the spectacular Niagara River gorge? Not if it means kids walking on my sidewalk to get there!

A fabulous new school on crumbling, largely abandoned Main Street? A project that could, just maybe, trigger a much-needed renaissance for the neighborhood bordering one of the world's greatest natural wonders? Unh-uh. Just think of the bus ride for those poor kids from the outskirts!

The community's leery attitude was fueled by the only hometown daily newspaper, the Niagara Gazette. A fixture in the Falls since the late 1800s and for decades, until very recently, a proud holding of the Gannett Group, the Gazette since 1997 has been operated by the significantly smaller — in stature, as well as in scope — Community Newspaper Holdings, Inc.

In the past, but particularly since becoming a CNHI "community" member, the Gazette had reveled in its role of community cynic, criticizing seemingly every public and private foray attempting to put the city back on the international tourist destination map.

The naysayer newspaper seemed to take particular delight in grumbling over the new high school project, vigorously protesting the very need for the project, while inexplicably failing to recognize the many and obvious advantages to the plan.

Those who relied upon the newspaper as their primary source of information were understandably cynical.

But even in the most unforgiving of climates, even in the most barren wastelands of apathy and apprehension, vision has been known to flourish, ideas to take bloom.

It's elementary, my dear Watson.

Or, in the case of the Niagara Falls City School District, it's secondary. As in schools.

Make that school.

Despite the initial apprehension and countless objections, a new Niagara Falls High School — one of the most state-of-the-art in all the land — has risen proudly from an overlooked and overgrown field. And it has risen from the most unlikely of circumstances: a ground breaking public-private partnership that has earned the blessing of elected officials and become tenuously embraced by the citizenry.

In true naysayer fashion, they've complained of everything from its placement to its size to its very name. But not one doom-and-gloomer — not a single, solitary one — has complained of increased tax bills as a result of the massive, $83 million project.

That's because taxes weren't raised one red cent to finance the project. Not one. Niagara Falls High School is a true first for New York State: a public school privately built, and done so entirely with private funds, in a unique lease-back arrangement. An educational edifice featuring all the latest and greatest bells and whistles, in the heart of a city that can ill afford to fill its many roadway potholes, much less fill the foundation for future growth.

Special governmental permission to issue Certificates of Participation (COPs) and use tax-free financing helped push the project over the economic hump. Sales tax and low-bid exemptions enabled the district to get the absolute most "bang for its buck."

The project represented a first in one other, extremely significant way: it was entirely union-built, yet done so beyond the prohibitive confines of the state's Wicks Law, which requires four prime contractors on all school and government projects. A controversial, one-time-only exemption was legislatively granted — an exemption that was closely monitored by labor groups and government officials alike, each dead-set on protecting their hard-earned gains and interests.

One miss-step on the Niagara Falls High School project could have effectively doomed future legislation for any and all similarly minded projects to follow.

Suffice to say, there were no stumbles.

Clearly, the Niagara Falls High School project did not come about quickly or easily. But the fact is, come about it did, and in incredibly grand fashion.

In a city where one man (former Mayor E. Dent Lackey) is generally credited with crippling a once-thriving downtown — with scaring off development and visitors and scores of residents alike in his zeal to "remake" Niagara Falls — one man had a vision of erecting a world-class educational center.

And of doing it without heightening the burden of an already overloaded taxpaying public.

Without further disrupting what's left of the prime tourist areas.

Without unduly provoking that NIMBY mentality.

Eschewing what could have been the most picturesque campus in all of the United States, on the lip of the lower Niagara River gorge, he opted for a site smack-dab in the middle of a polarized populace.

In an area where downstate legislators have habitually stood in the way of progress, as seen through Niagarans' eyes — namely, the legalization of casino gambling — one man confronted the system, that old-boy network winding snake like from Albany to all points beyond. He met them head-on, on their own turf, under their terms ... and he prevailed.

His name: Carmen Granto. Superintendent of schools, Niagara Falls, New York.

The path to the new Niagara Falls High School wound mainly through uncharted territories, yet Granto (and company) traversed it without the aid of so much as a compass. Trailblazing? We're talking Lewis and Clark caliber on this one. They pretty much wrote the manual as they went along.

Want to talk about getting it done? The Niagara Falls High School project raised the bar to dizzying new heights in terms of creative financing, circumventing legal obstacles and uniting traditional foes for the common good.

It redefined the phrase "thinking outside the box," both in terms of design and its paradigmatic integration of technology.

It set new standards in terms of overcoming significant community objection by giving citizens "ownership" of a project. Via community forums, face-to-face meetings or participation on committees setting policy and helping design the facility, any resident so inclined was given a voice in the final product. The result: it got done. And it got done in attention-grabbing fashion.

Architecture Week called the endeavor "a novel educational experiment (that) could well become a trend-setter for public schools in the United States. The technology built into the school promises to make it a world-class educational facility."

"An example of a true architecture, business, technology and community partnership developed as a result of needing to replace two aging high school facilities," raved The Architectural Record.

Even the New York Times took notice, publishing an in-depth, top-to-bottom examination of the project.

Granto's precedent-setting victory could very well represent the watershed mark in public education for years to come. Already, his efforts are being duplicated in the equally cash-strapped, Rust Belt sister-city of Buffalo, which saw his trailblazing work as a blueprint for upgrading that district's obsolete physical plants.

Numerous other school districts across the country have contacted Niagara Falls, seeking additional information and guidance.

In a larger, and also more personal sense, Granto's victory is being viewed by many as the spark, the catalyst, for the rebirth of his beloved hometown of Niagara Falls.

Uniting a divided populace with the erection of a single building? Pie-in-the-sky?

Not necessarily.

This isn't just any high school, you see. In fact, it's a school in only the strictest sense of the word, in that teaching and learning will take place within its four walls.

In other circles, to other people, it is other things.

It's a community forum, a convenient place to hold meetings. It's a recreational outlet, with a wide array of indoor and outdoor facilities available. It's a showplace, a venue for staging even the most elaborate events and productions.

It's a resource center, an outreach facility, a satellite office. You can go there for an education, to be certain. You can also drop in to get employment guidance, you can come by to get family counseling; the technologically challenged can even go there to get their feet wet surfing the world-wide web.

It is the future of Niagara Falls.

It is proof that vision and commitment can overcome apathy and skepticism, that the old ways are not necessarily the best ways, that the long-held sacred adage is, indeed, true: where there is a will, there is a way.

Evidence that the project triggered a "rebirth" of Niagara Falls is beginning to mount. In less than two years since the school's opening, two major initiatives have already been launched: the formation of a state-sponsored group to oversee resurrection of the nearly abandoned downtown — a la the acclaimed Times Square effort in New York City — and a landmark agreement with the Seneca Nation of Indians to finally bring casino gaming to the Falls and nearby Buffalo.

The gaming issue had been a political hot potato for 30 long years, bandied about and forwarded by an impressive succession of mayors and senators and assemblymen and even governors. Yet it had all the vital signs of an XFL franchise — had been thought dead, at least for the foreseeable future — until the NFHS project came along.

A coincidence of timing? Perhaps. Then again, the school focused the eyes of the nation — maybe even the world — upon Niagara Falls. What better time to put your best foot forward, to display all the other goodies you have to offer?

The "new" Niagara Falls High School. It is an amazing story. And it is real. Right in back yard, Niagara Falls, USA ... soon to be new and improved, itself.

And, as the Buffalo School District has already learned and others will no doubt eventually realize, it is also a geneticist's dream: readily cloned. You can have a new Niagara Falls High School of your very own — along with the many intangible benefits it can spawn — right in your own backyard. Here's the recipe ...

CHAPTER 1
IN THE BEGINNING

To say that germination of the Niagara Falls High School project occurred in the mid-1990s would be somewhat myopic. Granted, it was during that time frame that the seed was first planted in the minds of board members and taxpayers. But the groundwork, so to speak, had long since been done.

Arguably, the roots of the new school can be traced as far back as the mid-1950s, when the city was dealt a crushing blow courtesy of Mother Nature: a huge rock slide that wiped out an important hydroelectric generating facility.

That one event — lasting all of a few seconds — forever changed the face of Niagara. It triggered a series of events that altered both landscapes and mindscapes, properties and perceptions, eventually transporting weary Western New Yorkers down a storied path leading from feast to famine. Many scars from that tumultuous event remain to this very day ... some of which had major impact on the ultimate size, scope and significance of the NFHS project.

To fully appreciate the gravity and magnitude of the project — not only to the school district, but the community itself — it is necessary to dissect that sequence of events and to closely inspect the problems, politics and personalities it spawned.

The following, then, is a crash course examining "The Early History of Niagara Falls" complemented by the rather pathetic primer "Niagara Falls Politics 101."

First, a taste of Niagara as set forth in the history books ...

Located in Western New York some 20 miles north of Buffalo, Niagara Falls is separated from its sister city of Niagara Falls, Ontario by a rugged river that encompasses part of the easternmost United States-Canada border. The city took its name, of course, from the incredible cascading cataract effectively splitting the Niagara River into an "upper" strait and a "lower" gorge.

The river had been dubbed "Onguiaahra" (or On-Gi-Ara, literally "the neck") by the Native Americans who first called this place home. The region's permanent name was the result of hybridization of that moniker by early French explorers and subsequent British settlers.

The area's namesake river drains all four of the upper Great Lakes, directly connecting two of them — Erie to the south and Ontario to the north, hence the "neck" between two "bodies" reference. More accurately a "strait," the Niagara River flows some 35 miles before emptying into the Lake Ontario basin at Youngstown, New York, gaining substantial speed as it drops 326 feet in elevation over that distance.

The river is noteworthy in the fact that it is one of only seven rivers in the world to flow in a northerly direction. Featuring a stunning, huge "whirlpool" a short distance from the waterfall, the river also tends to momentarily reverse its flow at certain junctures, creating an unusual spectacle for nature lovers.

The waterway is central to the area's history, of course, for it was the preferred route of trade amongst early settlers, supplemented by the Ongiara Trail, a land route which circumvented the falls. Later, it provided the impetus for economic development: "New World" industrialists quickly recognized its potential and seized upon it as a source of inexpensive and unlimited energy.

Everything that is Niagara — past, present and future — stems from that unusual river and its awe-inspiring cliff.

HARNESSING THE POWER

In days past the Niagara River powered everything from saw mills to grain grinders and, in later incarnations, chemical plants and other manufacturing initiatives. It was via these enterprises that, over a mere half-century, Niagara Falls evolved from an isolated outpost to a bustling metropolis of some 100,000 people, recognized far and wide not only for its magnificent natural wonder, but for its unique contribution to mankind's technological advancement: Affordable, transmittable hydroelectric power.

Its blessed abundance of water — a full 25 percent of the earth's fresh water plummets over the precipice here — has in many ways defined Niagara since its incorporation as a city in

1892. It attracted such early pioneers as Nikola Tesla, whose "Tesla Coil" facilitated the first documented long-distance transmission of electricity, from Niagara Falls to Buffalo (1896).

Several prospective "power barons" tried their hands at harnessing the raging power of the Niagara. The Frenchman Daniel Joncaire was among the first; later settlers, employing water wheels, diverted small amounts of water to power their fledgling enterprises.

Blasting through layer upon layer of unyielding limestone, crews of workers began digging a hydraulic canal in 1853. The work wasn't completed for several years, and ultimately only one business, a flour mill, took advantage of its power opportunities. The property was subsequently sold to prospector Jacob Schoellkopf, who opened two additional mills along with a generating plant.

Eventually, several mills lined the upper lip of the Niagara gorge. Combined, they still utilized only a fraction of Niagara's potential, their watery discharges creating unsightly plumes down the gorge wall, like so many miniature waterfall wannabes.

In the 1880s, architect and naturalist Frederick Law Olmsted and businessman Thomas Evershed rather inadvertently teamed to turn Niagara Falls into one of the world's leading forces in hydroelectric power generation.

Olmsted pressed elected officials to preserve the integrity of the land around the falls, maintaining one of the world's natural wonders in its genuine state of pristine splendor. The New York State Legislature agreed with him, passing legislation in 1885 establishing the Niagara Reservation State Park. It is the oldest state park in the nation.

With the land directly above and below the falls targeted for preservation, the existing mills in the area had to be moved. And it was Evershed who offered mill owners hope with plans for an underground tunnel to funnel water from the upper to the lower river, where it would operate a powerful new invention: an advanced type of water wheel known as a turbine, capable of generating significantly more power than traditional water wheels.

Hundreds upon hundreds of workers took part in the construction of Evershed's canal and its accompanying generating plant. This influx marked the beginning of Niagara's boom period.

In the decades that followed, improvements and expansions turned Niagara into a key player in the energy game, with hydroelectric power generated at the city's Schoellkopf Power Plant eventually supplying much of the northeastern United States.

But on June 7, 1956, an ecological disaster threatened not only Niagara's standing as an energy giant, but it's very economic existence. A huge landslide down the face of the lower Niagara gorge wiped out much of the Schoellkopf plant; miraculously, only one worker died in the onslaught.

One hundred and twenty thousand tons of rock and soil rumbled down the chasm and onto the plant below. The catastrophe interrupted power production and consequently exposed the vulnerability of thousands of jobs, both in Niagara and along much of the eastern seaboard.

Many employers hastily left Niagara for greener pastures elsewhere, taking jobs and workers with them.

Quick and decisive action was necessary, and Congress responded by passing the Niagara Redevelopment Act. This move enabled the Federal Power Commission to license the New York Power Authority, the entity to be entrusted with building a new, world-class generating station at Niagara.

Once again, thousands of workers emigrated to the area and were employed digging a pair of huge underground conduits and a massive reservoir. Over 34 months they excavated some 10 million cubic yards of earth and an incredible 25 million cubic yards of rock, forever changing the gorge face in the process.

Thousands of others began work on the actual power plant itself, a colossal concrete tribute to technology which would bear the name of the man who oversaw its creation, Robert Moses. The skeleton of the 38-story plant consumed a whopping 3.7 million cubic yards of concrete.

Those conduits — each five miles long, 46 feet wide and 66 feet high — crisscrossed deep beneath the city to collectively shuttle 600,000 gallons of water each second to that lake-like, 22-billion gallon holding tank in the Town of Lewiston. At the adjacent Robert Moses Generating Plant, the water was then dropped 314 feet to spin 13 turbines and generate some 2.3 million kilowatts of electricity.

When it opened in 1961, the Niagara Project was the largest electricity producer in the Western world; it remains among the top five in the nation a full 40 years after its opening.

While the Niagara Power Project restored the area's standing as an energy icon, in the process preserving hundreds and perhaps thousands of local jobs, it did so at a considerable cost. Acre upon acre of prime waterfront and undeveloped suburban lands were placed under Power Authority jurisdiction, effectively eliminating hundreds of millions of dollars worth of land from the tax rolls and directly affecting both the current and more importantly the future coffers of Niagara Falls and the adjoining towns of Niagara and Lewiston.

Elected leaders sought recompense, but were largely rebuffed. Their reward was the plant itself, and the economic lifeline it represented. Its mission, as licensed by what is now the Federal Energy Regulatory Commission, was to not only preserve existing jobs but to facilitate — to produce — additional local employment for generations to come. It was an objective many in the area feel was never adequately achieved, and one which is being closely examined this very day, as the time approaches for renewal of the Power Authority's 50-year license.

Niagara's abundance of power was always a magnet for development. Industrialist Edward Acheson's Niagara Falls plant produced two abrasive products of his own invention: Carborundum and graphite. His Carborundum Company drew international acclaim for Niagara, as did other ventures, such as the Union Carbide Company, which produced electrochemicals used for bleaching and in the manufacture of the gas acetylene, and the Hooker Electrochemical Company, which produced caustic sodas, chlorine and other chemicals used worldwide.

Niagara's "industrial revolution" also included paper plants and the world-famous "Shredded Wheat" factory, later operated by Nabisco. With the influx of companies came an influx of people, and Niagara Falls burgeoned beyond the 100,000 point in population.

But there was a downside to all that development: pollution. It was over that dirty little word that Niagara's history and politics again clashed.

THE BOTTOM OF THE BARREL

With every manufacturing process there comes waste, and some of the wastes produced at Niagara were virtually unmatched in toxicity. Substances like dioxin and polychlorinated biphenyls (pcb's) represented deadly poison to humans. But in the 1930s and 1940s, science was not as exact as it is today. Disposal was not as carefully monitored as it is now. Many such wastes — including some of those from the U.S. Army's Manhattan Project (the atomic bomb) — were buried throughout the region, including tens of thousand of tons which were deposited into a dead-end trough known as the "Love Canal," after the man responsible for its never-completed construction.

Located in the city's LaSalle section, Love Canal was once a popular swimming spot for neighborhood children. Used largely by the Hooker Chemicals and Plastics Corporation for disposal of chemical waste, it was abandoned as a dump site in the early 1950s and was ultimately filled in, capped and given to the city in 1953.

An elementary school and a housing complex were subsequently built over the site. In fewer than 20 years, however, its toxic secrets began to be slowly and hideously revealed. Trees mysteriously died; vegetable gardens produced sickly yields. Eventually, chemical seepage reached the surface, triggering small fires and minor explosions. Traces of some 82 chemicals, including a number of known carcinogens, began to show up in nearby creeks, storm sewers and even residential basements.

The lasting legacy of Love Canal was horrifyingly revealed among its residents: in chromosomal damage linked to prolonged exposure to toxic chemicals; in an astounding number of birth defects and miscarriages; in alarming numbers of childhood nervous disorders, marked by seizures and other symptoms; and in higher-than-usual incidence of various cancers.

In 1978, Love Canal was declared a federal disaster area by then-President Jimmy Carter. Tens of millions of dollars were spent evacuating and relocating some 900 families. Hundreds of millions more have been spent to contain the damage from the nation's worst chemical waste-based environmental disaster, and ultimately rehabilitate the area to the point that much of its has now been repopulated.

In spite of initial denials of culpability — lawyers claimed, among other arguments, that the city and school district maneuvered to "force" Hooker to give up the canal land, even though company officials knew of its contamination and reportedly warned against its development — court cases have subsequently placed some, but not all of the blame, at the hands of the polluters.

The legal standoff has dragged on for decades and produced few clear winners; the economic fallout, however, was abrupt and unmistakable.

Many of those affected by the Love Canal crisis moved away from the area entirely, fearing for their health and safety. Residents became leery of the environment. Those undercurrents of anxiety rippled far and wide as the news spread, inflicting a calamitous blow to the city's new lifeblood: the tourism industry.

Traditional industry was adversely affected, as well. The ecological safeguards resulting from Love Canal made it economically prohibitive to dispose of industrial wastes; as a result, several businesses downsized, closed completely or relocated to regions considered more "business friendly."

Over the past quarter-century, those factors and others conspired to cost Niagara Falls a full one-third of its population. Now registering barely half of its peak 1960s population, the city struggles with an aged infrastructure supported by an equally aging population, over 60 percent whom are on fixed incomes or rely on some form of public assistance for daily survival, and who can ill afford the ever-increasing tax burden resulting from the population exodus.

Mike Kurilovitch

The direction of the city has changed dramatically from its early days as an industrial leader, to a more recent focus on tourism, service and hospitality. The "global village" of the 21st century opened new doors for Niagara — some of which were unceremoniously slammed shut by myopic leaders.

All of which brings us to the topic of politics and leadership, Niagara Falls-style ...

THE BLIND LEADING THE BLIND

"Falls Politics 101" is a voluminous tome perhaps more appropriately dubbed "How to lose population and influence developers (to peddle their wares elsewhere)." Sadly, it would be perfectly acceptable to substitute the terms "tax base" or "credibility" or even "status" in place of the more nondescript "population" of the subtitle, and the resulting phrase would be no less indicative of Niagara Falls' woes since the onset of "urban renewal" in the 1960s.

In a city built on the back of heavy industry, a prolonged exodus of manufacturing jobs set the stage for stagnation. Myopia and parochialism — commonly exhibited symptoms of the city's sometimes inept leadership — were just a couple of the dilemmas to have perpetuated the phenomenon, plaguing Niagara Falls for decades and eroding the territory like so many millions of gallons of raging, runaway water might systematically eat away a muddy precipice.

The natural progression of business, in which products become obsolete as other more dependable or affordable offerings enter the marketplace, took its toll on some of Niagara's industries. Rising costs of doing business, including a shortage of the area's notoriously cheap hydropower, did in others. The city's ill-advised, two-tiered tax system, in which businesses foot a much greater percentage of costs than homeowners, further cost jobs and is in the process of being overhauled.

Still, many Niagarans point to "urban renewal" when asked the source of the area's deep-seated problems.

Recognizing the city needed a facelift, officials set out in the mid 1960s to plot the overhaul. Spearheaded by then-Mayor E.

Dent Lackey, they searched for ways to update the old girl. Rather than a less-risky outpatient procedure, however, they opted for major, reconstructive surgery.

Culture and history were sacrificed in the name of "modernization." Neighborhoods were uprooted for the sake of aesthetic advancement. In one fell swoop the wrecking ball consumed some 1,000 homes and hundreds of small business places in the city's bustling South End, scattering the uprooted victims near and far.

A thriving downtown — once very much the rival of today's Niagara Falls, Ont. — was transformed into a mishmash of failed developments, unattractive attractions and one-way streets leading to ... well, nowhere.

Visitors had difficulty finding the very thing that brought them here in the first place: the falls. Instead, they were routed around a business district that seemed perpetually "under construction," yet offered rather slim pickings for their enjoyment. While the tourist area on the Canadian side of the falls literally teemed with traffic — its visitors intrigued by a honky-tonk menagerie of museums, ethnic eateries and family-oriented attractions — those staying on the American side found precious little to do after a day-trip to the nation's oldest state park. Their average stay dwindled to but a few hours, their typical financial outlays experiencing a similar nose dive.

The downtown that once bristled with foot traffic gradually disappeared. The huge retailers with their fancy window displays, the discount stores with the soda-fountain counters, the quaint souvenir shops: gone, either to the fancy shopping malls popping up in the suburbs, or else to retail heaven, just another Niagara Falls memory. In their place, an ugly concrete hulk of a convention center, perpetually mismanaged and grossly underutilized, never beginning to approach its promised potential in a city desperate for entertainment — not to mention the infusion of tourist dollars generated by conventions.

Mike Kurilovitch

The former Hart-To Hart Furniture store, Main Street, Niagara Falls, New York, vacant and boarded-up

Instead of glitzy amusements that captured the kids' eyes (and ultimately the family's discretionary dollars), downtown Niagara USA was saddled with "attractions" such as giant parking ramps, individually rising from the asphalt like some mammoth Phoenix arriving to save the sagging economy. Unfortunately, the evolutionary eyesores were more akin to the woolly mammoths of dinosaur-dom and likewise never delivered the expected revenues, quickly becoming obsolete.

Thus it was with the city's downtown water park; an idea that seemed good at the time, yet ultimately went the way of the Tyrannosaurus. In retrospect, perhaps an open-air water park in a locale enjoying (at best) maybe three months of summer-like weather per year was short-sighted. When it went under, the city was left holding the bag, and it was baggage with extremely limited attraction to investors. Hence, several prime downtown acres, situated on the fringe of what could and should rightfully have been a whirlwind tourist mecca, sit forlornly within tall fences, overgrown and deteriorating. The only action within: an occasional juvenile delinquent bent on further destruction. Visitors and residents alike can only drive by and wonder about the twisting towers arching above the skyline. In downtown Niagara USA, they are water slides only for random raindrops.

A succession of "leaders" have promised to put an end to the decline, most meeting with only marginal success — and some, none at all.

The Buffalo News recently wrote that Niagara Falls "has seen enough failed development plans to wallpaper the Niagara Gorge," everything from a downtown "mega-mall" to what amounted to an enclosed "carnival" to a cavernous night club. All have come and gone, leaving more blight in their wake: Empty shells and empty promises.

Another boarded-up downtown store: The former Jenss Department store on Main Street in downtown Niagara Falls, New York, long vacant

But it was "one that got away" that may have been the biggest blunder of all.

Mike Kurilovitch

In 1989, the nationally recognized Benderson Development company unveiled plans to construct a mammoth, $125 million factory outlet shopping mall at the edge of the city's downtown business district. It was a proposal that would have transformed over a hundred acres of decaying inner-city into a sprawling, discount-shopping mecca. The Mall of the (North) Americas.

Not only would it have meant a tremendous draw for cross-border shopping (Canadians at the time flocked here to stretch their ever-shrinking dollars) as well as an important attraction for visitors, it would have represented millions of dollars in tax revenue — not to mention hundreds of jobs, perhaps even thousands if the anticipated "spin-off development" were even partially realized.

Unlike an earlier proposal for a "mega-mall" in the same area, this one was seemingly legit: from a respected developer with solid local roots. But a climate of mistrust — fueled by years of official mismanagement, corruption and greed — conspired to undermine the project long before any shovels ever hit the ground.

Mayor Michael C. O'Laughlin had thrown his whole-hearted support behind the project, directing city officials to work out every minute detail with Benderson. Major tenants were lined up, funding streams were in place and peripheral developments were discussed. Niagara County and state government support was aligned. Every economic indicator pointed to tremendous potential for the city.

Then came the murmurs. An FBI investigation was targeting suspected fraud with past developments, and O'Laughlin's name had surfaced during the course of the probe.

Corruption: another sadly familiar face to long-time Niagarans, many of whom can tick off a list of project after project to have been riddled with fraud. For some even the developers' names remain fresh, having become synonymous locally with deception and greed.

Strangely, some of those very same names continue to crop up, again and again — like some stubborn, pesticide-resistant weed — each time with a "newfangled" proposal, routinely gaining the undivided attention of the latest batch of gullible council members and administrators.

Getting It Done

O'Laughlin, a former school teacher and administrator, had managed to maintain an unblemished reputation when it came to such shenanigans, but this time the rumors were proving more difficult to shake.

Opponents naturally made political hay with the situation and the aging and ailing O'Laughlin decided to forego another reelection bid after 16 years in the mayor's chair.

His eventual successor, former firefighter and union boss Jacob A. Palillo, ran long and hard with the corruption allegations. He promised accountability and pledged to be a hard-nosed negotiator when it came to developers bent on ripping off the city. He formulated his campaign around his suspicions that city taxpayers would once again be left holding the financial bag were the mega-mall project to become a reality.

On Nov. 5, 1991, Palillo edged out Benderson mall (and O'Laughlin) supporter Anthony Quaranto in what was believed to have been the closest mayoral election in city history.

Palillo's political rise expedited the fall of the Benderson mall plans. O'Laughlin was subsequently exonerated of any wrongdoing, and a downsized Factory Outlet Mall project went to a grateful Town of Niagara, mere miles from its planned site in the Honeymoon City.

A view of the main entrance to the Prime Outlets Mall in the Town of Niagara, originally proposed for the City of Niagara Falls

OPPORTUNITY LOST

Today the Benderson mall houses hundreds of factory outlets for such internationally recognizable names as Polo, Ralph Lauren, Saks and Tommy Hilfiger, and draws a steady stream of visitors, many of whom come by the bus load, particularly during holiday periods.

A view of the main parking area for the Prime Outlets Mall in the Town of Niagara

A street running adjacent to the convention center has since been renamed in honor of the now-deceased O'Laughlin, testament to the man's contributions during his four terms in office. Town of Niagara officials were said to have privately toyed with the idea of similarly recognizing Palillo for his more "indirect" contributions to the town's good fortunes, but the idea hit a dead end — much the same as Palillo's mayoralty did at the completion of his lone term.

Getting It Done

The proposed mall site in downtown Niagara USA? Today it remains a collection of unkempt houses, overgrown lots and empty space — coincidentally bordering the aforementioned convention center, and but a stone's throw from the similarly situated splash park. Even the gaping spaces designated as overflow "parking" for the gambling casino since erected right across the river in Niagara Falls, Ont., sit largely empty, idle and ignored.

The largely abandoned area once planned for a Niagara Falls Mega-Mall.

Much of the mall's anticipated "peripheral" development also ended up in the Town of Niagara, which continues to reap the significant financial benefits. Meanwhile, the City of Niagara Falls plunged deeper and deeper into economic gloom, desperate for something — anything — that would turn the tables.

"We remain a community watching our neighbors — in particular Canada — just bulge at the seams," remarks longtime community activist and school board member Don King. "We have many of the same players, and the same natural ingredient: the falls. Yet we lag behind. There's something wrong."

As the new millennium dawned — and short of the long hoped-for casinos — the best bet for liberating Niagara Falls from its dismal past rested with the new high school, seen by many as a symbol for the area's eagerly anticipated rebirth.

"I consider it the jump-start for renewal that the private sector hasn't been able to generate," King said. "They've offered a lot of plans, but they haven't come to fruition. What better way to bring a community together than through its school system?"

OPPORTUNITY FOUND

A school board member for the better part of the last three decades, King has been simultaneously saluted and scorned in his hometown. Some see him as visionary — idealistic, perhaps, but a mover nonetheless — while others view him as administrative putty, a mere rubber stamp for his "hand-picked" superintendent.

His accomplishments speak for themselves, however, and they speak volumes.

In volunteer capacities, he has seen both the Niagara Falls Memorial Medical Center and the Niagara Falls Public Library through some extremely trying times.

Both are now on the rebound.

King was not about to be led by the nose on the high school proposal. He was tentative with his approval at first, weighing the many pros and cons. In the end, however, he simply could not overlook the fact that the project made perfect sense on so many levels, not the least of which was financially, but also educationally and, in a broader sense, in terms of community.

King can now proudly add Niagara Falls High School to his impressive list of personal success stories — perhaps with even bigger fish awaiting down the road.

"The timing was very crucial for the redevelopment of Niagara Falls," King said. "People-wise, shaping attitudes ... We gave our kids the arena in which to be competitive with others around the world. We can compete, facility-wise, with any school in the country. Our kids don't have to be second-best any more. Then it all goes back to the community, and changing attitudes ... this was school politics at its best."

But was it truly the shining example of community development educational leaders would like citizens to believe?

Granted, the new school most definitely will not extend the average stay for visitors — unless they just happen to be among the legions of educators arriving regularly to tour the new facility, to study its design, to see its innovative programs in action. Or, they just happen to be among the everyday folks participating in weekend sporting or cultural events in the school's gymnasium or pool, or taking in any of the number of programs offered regularly in the building's performing arts center.

Likewise, it most likely will not lighten the tax burden for citizens — unless, of course, one considers that this $83 million marvel was achieved at absolutely *no additional cost* to those taxpayers, an accomplishment which would be viewed by those in the "glass half-full" camp as a tax savings.

Nor will the new school pad the city's tax rolls — unless it does act as a catalyst for development, with companies deciding to build or relocate in Niagara Falls in part because of the presence of a world-class school system, among other attractive benefits.

Will it bring much-needed jobs to the area? Not per se — unless that "trigger" effect is realized. Can it possibly improve the housing stock, or fill empty units? See previous answers for a clue to that one.

How about rejuvenating a sickly downtown area? Again, not without some spin-off development. We can be fairly certain, however, that maintaining the previously existing two school buildings wouldn't have made one iota's difference for any of these critical concerns.

Will the new school in some way help to diminish poverty, reduce crime, or increase the availability of low-cost power so vital for keeping what industry remains and attracting any new investment?

Don't discount the possibility out-of-hand. Consider that:

Mike Kurilovitch

Having sensed the urgency of the situation — and having seen the major commitment undertaken by the local school board — New York Governor George Pataki in 2001 pledged to rescue downtown Niagara USA. He intends to accomplish this a la the well-documented reversal of fortunes achieved for New York City's Times Square: by offering incentives to attract development, by lending monies and critical expertise to see to it that things happen, by helping to negotiate a brighter future.

And then there's the long-awaited casino, which has the community buzzing ... and prospective developers tripping over each other to get in line for a piece of the pie.

A view of the main entrance to the new Seneca-Niagara Casino in Niagara Falls, New York, which officially opened on Dec. 31, 2002

Could it all be just a major coincidence of timing? Would it have happened anyway, had they simply patched the roof and replaced the windows and maintained the status quo at the old Niagara Falls and LaSalle high schools?

That's for all the pundits and all the analysts and each Niagaran to judge for themselves.

Getting It Done

Already, however, one can sense the spirit of excitement brewing.

Voters once disillusioned to the point of disgust — whose friends and neighbors voted with their feet in moving from the area en masse — see potential for the city once again. In some circles, it might even be characterized as optimism — a rare commodity in these parts, indeed.

And much of that hope, much of that promise springs skyward — about four stories skyward, to be exact — from a site at 4455 Porter Road.

Granted, that's an awful lot to expect, an awful lot to hope for from what amounts to roughly 400,000 square feet of bricks and mortar.

Then again, as previously noted, this is not just ANY new school.

CHAPTER 2
BACK TO THE FUTURE

The "super-school" that is Niagara Falls High obviously didn't happen overnight. Construction alone consumed a full two years, but that represents only the tip of a Titanic-sized iceberg. Between talking, planning, trouble-shooting and implementation stages, the process consumed a full decade, and then some.

Once it was determined that the city's two existing high schools would be closed and merged into a new school (a time-consuming matter in itself that will be covered in greater detail later in this chapter), intense lobbying and negotiations commenced at the state level; first to convince legislators that a privately funded public school project could work, and next to seek critical legislative remedies to the many obstacles that may have foiled its success.

There's an old blues standard called "Five Long Years" and in this case it was all of that, and then some — a grueling process that, without diligence, easily could have doomed the project at any number of junctures.

Next, of course, came the dealings with prospective developers, architects, contractors and the like, each complicated by the distinctive nature of the project. Nothing was routine along the path to the new NFHS.

Sessions followed with community groups determined to have a say in the process. Homeowners dead-set against a school in their neighborhood; business owners focused on averting another tax increase; even Little League moms bent on protecting their kids' recreational turf.

It was a veritable obstacle course of opposition, occasionally forcing district officials into a conciliatory tap dance.

In the interim, a pair of action teams were assembled and worked diligently for many months to make recommendations: one focusing on what should be done, facility-wise, and (later) another examining how the new school should look and how it would operate.

Teachers and administrators sat side-by-side with students, parents and community leaders. There was no hierarchy; everyone's opinion counted the same.

The Senior High School Site Selection and Evaluation Committee ("SHEC," appointed by the school board in February, 1994) assumed responsibility for evaluating two critical aspects: educational program needs for senior high students of the 21st century, and structural needs for the dilapidated Niagara Falls High.

They would help determine the answer to the pivotal question: renovate or rebuild?

Including leaders from the religious community, higher education, city government, even the Chamber of Commerce, the team was given free reign, but with one important caveat: it was absolutely imperative that both considerations be addressed with the understanding that they be accomplished with as little impact as possible — preferably NONE — on local taxpayers.

So the edict for SHEC was clear: without worrying about money, get us out of this facility dilemma. But keep in mind that there is no money with which to do much of anything ...

Yeah, right.

Coming along much later in the process — in February, 1998, after the "rebuild" decision had been reached — the High School Quality Council ("HSQC") inherited an equally simple, yet complex charge: now that the facility dilemma had been resolved, they had to determine how the new school would operate, program-wise.

Splitting into four teams, HSQC members studied "context, content, learning and teaching" elements — in other words, they researched the best practices, programs and services available for the new school. Each team developed a list of ideas designed to shape the programs to be offered. Dozens upon dozens of these suggestions were ultimately incorporated into the school's action plan, dealing with everything from the physical environment to the school day to the teaching process itself.

Mike Kurilovitch

"The staffs from both high schools — the users — essentially designed the whole building," Granto said. "They got 98 percent of what they wanted. The rest just wasn't feasible."

HSQC put its indelible and highly personalized stamp upon the program, an undeniably unique gesture that fostered a sense of "ownership" while molding the project to more seamlessly fit its community. It was, indeed, one of the crowning glories of the project, but more on that later ...

The entire process culminating in the "super" NFHS followed a clearly scripted process Granto and the board had put into place shortly after his hiring in 1992, specifically for dealing with such weighty issues.

The methodology: extensive research and study, followed by meaningful public input, and topped by careful staff analysis of any resulting concerns. Superintendent makes recommendation to board, board votes, process completed.

Exceedingly simple, extremely effective.

Clearly, the Niagara Falls High project consumed incredible amounts of time and thought, inspiration and perspiration. It all began with a pair of aging buildings, some glaring maintenance problems, a shortfall of cash, and an overriding desire to do right by the children of a community, regardless of the monumental barriers standing in the way.

WHERE IT ALL BEGAN

As Spanish-born poet, philosopher and novelist George Santayana (1863-1952) quite succinctly noted, "Those who cannot remember the past are condemned to repeat it."

There is a very valid reason, after all, why history is taught in our schools; why it is such a critical element in any educational undertaking. That reason is really quite simple, as Santayana noted: In order to fully comprehend and appreciate the events of the day — and in doing so, reap greater benefit from our future — we must be well-versed on the events of our past.

In other words, you can't know where you're going if you don't know where you've been.

Getting It Done

Those who succeed in this life do so by avoiding the mistakes of the past, and by anticipating the obstacles of the future.

With that as their dictum, the movers and shakers central to the Niagara Falls High School project set forth intent on blazing new trails in education. Their goal was much more than a sparkling new building in which to practice the same tired routines. They knew this project represented a golden opportunity — the once-in-a-lifetime variety, perhaps — of changing the face of education, of impacting the future.

As such, everything was deemed fair game, from the physical plant to the academic program to the school calendar to the very environment itself. After all, what would be accomplished by erecting a state-of-the-art educational facility incorporating a calendar geared toward the farmer's prime growing season? Or a daily schedule built around the fantasy of family dinner at 4 p.m.? It was just such antiquated ideals — with roots as old as the original NFHS, yet still widely and routinely practiced — that organizers wanted put out to pasture, once and for all.

Such practices will soon be going the way of the Edsel and the eight-track tape, courtesy of the visionary folks charged with planning a new Niagara Falls High School.

NFHS 2001, as you will come to see, is a living, breathing, adaptive entity, a model for schools of the 21st century. It represents the evolution of education, with its flexible schedules, its global mind set, its unparalleled involvement of community. It is total access, pure and simple. Those seeking knowledge and in search of truth, those exploring the boundaries of modern life — all can find it here, within these very walls. Limitations cease upon entry. It is the doorway to the future, and a boundless future it promises to be.

NFHS 2001 is a grand accomplishment. It is so, to a large degree, because those entrusted with making it so recognized the importance of history. They did their homework, so to speak; paid attention to detail. They closely examined mistakes of the past, took copious note of today's successes, and even glanced into the future, projecting trends to achieve a more accurate picture of what the city would be like — and what

Mike Kurilovitch

exactly would be expected of its "new" high school — five, 10, even 20 years down the road.

They used all that knowledge, all that information, to assure that NFHS 2001 would be — to borrow a phrase from the Army — all it could be.

It all began with SHEC — or, to borrow a more appropriate tag from an equally prominent event, the NFHS "Dream Team." They were the original trailblazers, and logically, their quest began with a quick jaunt in the proverbial time machine ...

THE GHOSTS OF NFHS PAST

The countdown — to the new NFHS, that is — started at three. As recently as 1988 the city maintained three separate and distinct high schools: The original NFHS, of course (believed to have been the oldest operating high school in the country); LaSalle Senior High, located on the outskirts of the city; and a third, more centrally located facility, named after the late James Fullerton Trott.

Trott had been a founding member of the city's school board and ultimately served for a full half-century, continuously, earning him well-deserved recognition as "The Father of Niagara Falls Schools."

The Trott facility was dedicated on March 11, 1929, a secondary school committed strictly to vocational pursuits.

In his dedication address, Dr. Lewis A. Wilson, then the assistant commissioner for vocational education, noted that secondary education had historically been formulated in such a manner as to academically prepare "the more fortunate among us who planned to enter college." He said that Trott Vocational would instead be geared to "the 90 percent of children" who would never go to college.

Keep in mind, we're talking Depression-era here.

"We are interested in the development of an educational program organized to meet the social needs of the community," Wilson said. Trott Vocational would "prepare many boys and girls to meet the ever-increasing demands of industry and commerce," as well as "prove an aid to thousands of adults who must secure additional training to keep abreast of changing industrial conditions, or those who wish to prepare for a better position in industry and commerce."

Spoken some 70 years ago, yet the sentiment remains as fresh as a just-trimmed rose. But that's the way history is; sometimes, the more things change ... the more they stay the same.

"Trott," as it came to be known, was a three-story brick structure located just a few blocks down Portage Road from the hallowed halls of NFHS — or, as it was more simply referred to within the community, "high school." In its heyday Trott housed 43 classrooms in which students received basic core-subject instruction, complimented by intensive course work in the fundamentals of specialized pursuits ranging from cosmetology to welding, from electronics to auto repair.

On-site "shops" allowed students to sharpen their skills under real-life settings and conditions. For many years, Trott Vocational proudly turned out proficient graduates ready to enter the skilled-labor work force.

But gradually, as the workplace evolved into a more technologically advanced place, increasing numbers of students recognized the importance of post-secondary education. Trott's numbers began to dwindle, and programs such as drafting and practical nursing were ultimately relocated to NFHS. In 1988, the school board — citing obsolescence as its primary reason, along with a desire to cut costs — decided to close Trott, moving its remaining programs to brand-new facilities on the LaSalle campus.

LaSalle, after all, was a much more modern facility, having opened in 1957. It originally housed 72 classrooms, with a subsequent addition tacking on 11 more. A 1970 expansion, complemented by another $8 million project in 1988, created spacious quarters for instruction in automotive repair, carpentry, electronics, machinery, welding and horticulture.

With its modern design, capitalizing on a profusion of natural lighting and highlighted by a state-of-the-art auditorium capable of seating some 1,400 people, LaSalle became the district's showcase school, hosting countless important community events.

Mike Kurilovitch

But if LaSalle was the district's showcase, Niagara Falls High was its centerpiece. Arriving on the scene in 1903 to "centralize" earlier operations (then-Superintendent Nathaniel L. Benham believing a single site to be more economically feasible than continuing with the two existing high schools — sound familiar?) the building rose at the busy intersection of Pine Avenue and Portage Road at a cost of some $150,000.

The up-and-coming town quickly outgrew those original accommodations, however, and in 1920 a $325,000 annex was approved. It was during construction of that project that a fire ripped through the building on January 24, 1922, leveling much of the original complex.

While school officials scrambled to locate temporary housing for classes, work on the annex continued without interruption, and it was completed within a year. The gutted shell of the initial structure was demolished and rebuilt, opening to much fanfare some 18 months later.

An exterior view of the "old" Niagara Falls High School, now an arts center housing studio and gallery space for local artists

Getting It Done

Achieved at a cost of some $1.3 million, the original "new" Niagara Falls High School boasted "every modern, educational convenience known to the era," local historian Patricia Rice wrote in chronicling the history of the Falls' schools. At the time, it was considered one of the finest high school buildings in the state, she noted.

Ah, the more things change ...

The building was renovated in 1963 to accommodate the population influx created by construction of the giant Robert Moses Niagara Power Project. Residents took great pride in the final product, with its handsome facade featuring six stately stone pillars; its opulent auditorium boasting fancy ironwork and ornate ceiling; and its luxurious library, laid out in rich tones of choice oak veneer.

THAT WAS THEN, THIS IS NOW

With that little history lesson in hand, the NFHS Dream Team members reentered their time machine, this time to gain a better perspective on the very recent past. Destination: late 20th century.

Although a relatively brief jaunt, time-wise, it is as if entering an entirely different dimension in terms of the two high schools. Vastly different pictures of both NFHS and LaSalle emerged:

Having reached the big 4-0, LaSalle is definitely beginning to show its age. Ceramic tiles peel from the walls; once-elegant sections of laminated wood begin to separate. Toilet facilities have become obsolete, windows are in disrepair and asbestos is rampant throughout the facility.

But those problems are small potatoes compared to those at NFHS, which comes across as a grand old building which has served its community well, but has likewise suffered terribly at the hands of Father Time.

It becomes clear that the ravages of rugged northeastern winters have exacted a toll. The building's original flat roof proved a bane to school officials, springing more leaks than the proverbial little Dutch Boy's dike. What once was a seasonal event later became commonplace: If it rained or snowed outside, it did likewise within.

A cursory glance might give observers the impression the gymnasium is a cutting edge athletic facility — the kind with a retractable roof. Problem is, that hole big enough to drive a team bus through can't be closed on command. It's the kind that results from years of cumulative water damage. Sadly, that same gymnasium represents the landlocked school's solitary on-site athletic facility — but the leaky roof prevents the school from staging its basketball games there.

"The district actually had basketball games that were rained out," Granto says with incredulity.

As a result of the gymnasium's condition, NFHS home basketball games are, curiously enough, played at LaSalle — which creates an unusual situation, indeed, when the foe is that same LaSalle team (a perennial state powerhouse, by the way).

SHEC members learn that periodic repairs were undertaken, with varying degrees of success. Ultimately, the design flaws proved to be of a magnitude beyond the district's resources. With a half-million dollars per year targeted at maintaining just this one of the district's fleet of buildings, good money was being spent after bad in fruitless attempts to alleviate the problem. Roof replacement loomed as a $1 million Band-Aid for a patient desperately in need of a transplant.

By the time the 1990s rolled around, school board members and district administration had grown weary of throwing money at the problem and began to seek alternative solutions — i.e., a major overhaul, if not a new building entirely.

By this time, a trip down the school's dank hallways (which now consisted of no less than eight different levels, due to the various renovations) had became more like a trek into the Carlsbad Caverns:

Huge, jury-rigged sheets of plastic were suspended from leaky spots in the ceiling like so many stalactites, the runoff from above slowly trickling down to the floor where ...

Plastic trash receptacles jutted up like intermittent 50-gallon stalagmites, receiving said runoff and storing it safely for proper disposal at a later time.

Getting It Done

A peek inside a nearby classroom confirms that these alien beasts are prolific; another one has, in fact, reproduced between desks and chalkboard, interrupting traffic flow and distracting learners.

Occasional glances upward reveal steel skeletons of framework, wads of wiring and wrapped pipes, all laid bare by ceiling tiles which have long since succumbed to the relentless runoff.

At a critical point our gaze is directed toward a gap that creates a virtual "planetarium" effect: We can see clear through to the sky!

Other points bring other revelations: Broken and rusted lockers, ill-lit (and in some cases dead-end) hallways, God-forsaken opaque windows ...

Emerging into the light of day, we find that the deterioration is not limited to the interior. In the shadows of those famous pillars lie the equivalent of two flights of narrow concrete stairs leading to the main doors. Some are cracked, others crumbly, testament to the rigors of northern winters. Winters that, coincidentally, transformed the usually agreeable ascent into a slushy, slippery stroll.

While it is that rudimentary "aqueduct" system which draws the most attention, the aforementioned windows run a close second.

A WINDOW ON THE WORLD

Oddly — and however unwelcome — those internal water works may have provided the only clues as to external weather conditions for many students. Their daytime linkages to the outside world had long since been clouded, you see, by Lexan (plexiglass) windows lining two sides of the building which aged had into an opaque finish, like giant cataracts on the eyes of the aging building.

Initially installed to deter window vandalism, the plexiglass portals did the trick in that regard. The useful shelf life of the plexiglass was fleeting, however, and within a few short years it was not only deflecting wayward rocks, but also sunlight. Entire portions of the building were not only cut off from natural light, but from visual contact with the world beyond the windows.

Granted, in certain circles that may not have been viewed as being entirely bad; some might argue that it effectively curtailed student daydreaming. Although it was certainly not how district officials would have preferred to operate a high school, they nonetheless balked at the expensive proposition of replacing the costly fixtures a second time within such short proximity.

That reluctance to write blank checks for the care of a critically ill patient (keep in mind that the cost of major renovations such as roof repair did not qualify for the usual 83 percent reimbursement from the state) struck Dream Team members as very revealing — explaining in some measure how the original NFHS building deteriorated to the point of becoming a potential health hazard.

In that very important respect — safety — they learned that the LaSalle building lagged not far behind.

By the mid-1990s, the physical condition of the city's two remaining high schools had become a major concern for board members and district officials alike, particularly in the wake of a study by the New York State United Teachers union suggesting that "sick buildings" were becoming increasingly responsible for the number of sick students and staffers.

The authors of the study blamed poor air circulation for dust buildup and concentration of toxic fumes emitted from products such as new carpets, insecticides, floor waxes and room deodorizers. Leaky roofs contributed to mold problems.

The study noted that wildly fluctuating temperatures resulted from faulty and obsolete thermostats and other control devices in school buildings, creating uncomfortable environs not conducive to learning.

These conditions contributed to a plethora of allergy and flu-like symptoms, officials warned. Niagara Falls High, in particular, and LaSalle Senior, to a lesser degree, suffered from many of the problems outlined in the report.

At LaSalle, for instance, students and staffers alike complained of odors from the automotive program, saying exhaust fumes choked off hallways and even seeped into classrooms. Incidents of dizziness and lightheadedness were investigated.

The level of concern mounted inside each building, which led to the ultimate debate: what to do about it all?

And that, friends, is how the Dream Team (or SHEC if you prefer — those hardy souls entrusted with deciding what to do about the whole situation) came to be in the first place.

TO FISH OR CUT BAIT?

In trying to reach a decision on whether to renovate existing buildings, rethink and retool or simply relocate and start from scratch, SHEC-ies took numerous factors into consideration. Aside from the obvious — age and condition of the existing buildings and the costs inherent with each proposal — they also had to consider the community itself and its ability to see any potential plan through to fruition.

All the Clairol products in the world couldn't hide Niagara Falls' graying: the 1990 United States census revealed over 25 percent of the city's population to be age 60 or over, with a large percentage of those folks subsisting upon fixed incomes.

In fact, 13 percent of ALL city households received public assistance, a figure nearly double the state average, while nearly 16 percent of the population existed on incomes falling at or below the federal poverty level. The average Niagaran's household income of $20,641 represented only about 60 percent of the statewide average.

Keep in mind, too, that over 70 percent of the city's taxpaying public had no children in the school system ... and it was quite clear that property tax increases were out of the question; simply beyond the means of the vast majority of taxpayers.

Recognizing that fact, the administration and school board had already held the line on tax increases for five consecutive years (a figure currently at 10 and counting), and Granto realized that even a desperate need for a new school building could not alter that stance.

Likewise, Granto and Co. had to consider the future outlook for the city. A bustling metropolis it was no more. The Niagara

Falls of the late 20th century was burdened with some of the highest unemployment rates in the entire state. To say that local taxes were cumbersome was an understatement of mythical proportions. It was those very taxes, in fact, which were often cited as THE motivating factor for companies fleeing the area, and by the Mom-and-Pop shops closing the doors of businesses which had previously sustained the city — and their families — for untold decades.

That exodus had understandably taken a toll on the city. The tax base was dwindling, as were taxpayers, themselves. Population over a 40-year period had shrunk by nearly half from its one-time level of 100,000. District projections called for a continued decline, with the biggest dip coming amongst those of school age. School enrollment had already plummeted from a high of 19,000 students to slightly over 9,000, with continued losses projected.

So it was abundantly clear that any resolution to the schools issue had to come without major cost to those stubborn-but-struggling folks left behind. It was Granto and Co.'s mission to find a way to make it happen.

So when SHEC first floated the idea of renovating or rebuilding, reaction was understandably skeptical. Either way, the price tag would start at roughly $11 million and only climb from there. Estimates for repairing and renovating NFHS alone ran as high as $40 million — an ungodly sum that would result in putting a new face on an old building, while still having to deal with insufficient room, inadequate facilities for the handicapped and inferior technological capabilities.

Small wonder, then, why certain pockets of the community questioned the advisability of such a plan. Others, however, had to concede that something had to be done about the existing programs and facilities.

So, would it be renovation or rebuilding?

Or ... the district could start from scratch and figure out a way to correct those deficiencies while consolidating the two existing schools into one — possibly at one of the existing sites, or perhaps in an entirely new building at a site to be determined.

Of course, it would have to be done in such a way as to fall within the economic means of a community ill-prepared to deal with such potentially paralyzing financial consequences.

No small feat.

It turned into an issue that divided the city like the very boundary for those two high schools. There were those who wanted change, there were those who refused to let go of the past. Those who wanted new, those who saw nothing wrong with the old.

There were "LaSalle" people and there were "high school" people — factions who felt that, as Kipling once said — "never the twain shall meet."

Behind them were those who tentatively supported a merger, yet feared the unknown: What would happen when two traditional rival factions were thrown together within the same building? Would there be civil war?

Mostly, however, there were those who feared the economic implications of any resolution, regardless of whether it entailed renovation, rebuilding or relocating anew.

They were buoyed by critics who charged the school board and administration with furthering their cause for a new building by way of "planned obsolescence" of the existing facilities. By allowing both high schools to deteriorate, the case for building new would be bolstered, they argued. After all, why sink tens of millions of dollars into a pair of obsolete buildings when, for roughly the same money, a new "super school" could be had?

The Niagara Gazette, in a 1996 editorial, noted that there were a "number of buildings in the city that have withstood the years handsomely through preventive maintenance and capital expenditures when needed. Although Niagara Falls High School is structurally sound, critics say the years — and the school district — have not been kind to the building."

The paper went on to call the building "neglected," saying that it needed "an aggressive maintenance and capital improvement program, not consignment to planned obsolescence."

Mike Kurilovitch

CONSPIRACY THEORIES

Many in the community formulated their own conspiracy theory, speculating that repairs were intentionally neglected to further the cause for a new school.

Not true ... yet not completely removed from the truth.

"The fact of the matter is, the building was maintained minimally over time," said former principal Robert DiFrancesco. "Enough to keep the building safe, but to be honest, on the big issues there was neglect over time."

With budgets going ever upward and enrollment numbers heading in the opposite direction, DiFrancesco admitted that "budgets were balanced on the back of Niagara Falls High School."

"People wanted to know who let the building go to hell. They wanted to blame Carmen Granto," DiFrancesco said. "I told them to look at his predecessors."

One letter from a prominent citizen summed up residents' feelings: "I suggest the board spend more time analyzing a preventive maintenance program than a new school," it suggested. "I don't think the community can afford any such structure."

By way of reasoning, this individual cited the case of the Kansas City, Missouri school district, claiming that its board spent $1.2 billion updating facilities and subsequently "saw academic standards nose dive."

"Please do not take this letter as unsympathetic to the students," the writer continued. "They deserve better — but it has also been noted that a new school or updated facilities has nothing to do with academics."

The Gazette (again) checked in with its own opinion: scaled-down renovation.

"We (call) on the school district to consider an option it has not previously discussed in the eight years of studying whether to renovate, consolidate or build new. We (ask) how much it ~uld cost to repair the worst parts of the existing building, do ˑ˗ scaled-down renovation project and improve the

The paper also called for the district to seek a waiver from "the expensive proposition of bringing the entire building up to new state standards."

Clearly, business leaders were not siding with those pushing for a new school. They submitted a laundry list of questions and concerns, clearly outlining their preference for the less financially burdensome option of renovating the existing sites.

The newspaper clearly appeared to favor taking the cheapest way out, not even bringing the building up to standard in terms of classroom size, much less addressing issues such as handicapped accessibility. Technological innovation wasn't even on its menu.

By June, 1996, the school board had narrowed the field of options from nine to two: a new school at one of two potential sites, or a limited expansion of the existing Niagara Falls High. Per its established process, studies continued.

Granto's charge now would become to gauge the sentiment of the general public. They were the ones who would foot the bulk of the bill, after all. He wanted to know what they thought, and he wanted to hear it directly from their mouths.

He would take his lead from them.

CHAPTER 3
LEADING BY EXAMPLE

Although he might prefer a moniker more along the lines of "Godfather" — a movie favorite he references frequently for comic effect — those closest to Granto use a couple other adjectives in describing his persuasive powers and leadership style.

It's purely a matter of perspective, of course. But whether one prefers "politician" or "diplomat," the end result is usually the same. The man is a charmer with an incontestable knack for A. getting people to see (and subsequently buy in to) his point of view and B. drawing the very best from those same people once they do.

He's also a tactician, deal-maker, community servant and, most importantly, educator. It's a combination of qualities which have served him well in his 30-plus year career, the past dozen of which have been spent as superintendent. In that role he has become a world-class juggler, serving a variety of masters with a steady hand, an unflinching eye and a keen sense of balance.

Throw in a touch of a bulldog blood — lending those inherent traits of toughness and tenacity — and you have Carmen Granto.

Every one of those characteristics came in handy, and were put to good use, during the protracted NFHS ordeal.

Unlike many of his contemporaries on the city side of government, however, Granto doesn't make his decisions in a vacuum. A dictator he most certainly is not. Where they have failed in their autocratic ways, he has succeeded with democracy. With their reluctance to build bridges, they have constructed a series of dead-ends, leading their constituents nowhere. Granto, on the other hand, has utilized that uncanny ability to draw the very best from those around him in order to bridge gaping chasms and realize unparalleled victories. The new NFHS is merely the latest — albeit the most impressive — example.

Granto the Hun? Hardly. In fact, the Granto administration ushered in a new era of employee trust and empowerment to Niagara Falls schools. He introduced such concepts as shared decision-making and total quality management, delegating authority and placing trust in his chosen leaders to solve the vast majority of school-related problems at the individual building level.

In the lexicon of the 12-step programs, Granto is an "enabler." His faith in his team enables individual members to excel. The "trickle-down" process carries that faith, that belief, to the deepest levels of the organization.

If not the incredible new high school, then the immeasurable endowment of "empowerment" has to be considered the enduring hallmark of the Granto regime.

That glowing opinion may be commonly held within the confines of the school system. Beyond its boundaries, however, that basic mistrust of government still flourishes within the community — in some cases extending to the school district administration via guilt-by-association.

That's the type of mind set a decade of quasi-dictatorial leadership promotes. A trio of power-hungry mayors clashing with equally compulsive councilmen and accomplishing absolutely nothing in the process terminally tainted the public's faith in its elected representation.

Nevertheless, Granto knew that in order to accomplish his objectives and successfully resolve the high school issue, he had to traverse the trickiest of terrains — winning over a pessimistic public.

In embarking on the potentially risky endeavor of inviting public input on the school issue, some in the community probably expected Granto to employ a popular "political" tack: Stacking the deck. Sleight of hand. The old shell game.

But that was not and is not Granto's style. A longtime and very vocal proponent of allowing "stake holders" their say in the educational process, he promised the public a voice, and that's exactly what was delivered.

And a monumental move it proved to be.

Mike Kurilovitch

THE VOICE OF THE PEOPLE

Clearing his schedule as much as possible in order to take the role of point man, Granto promptly scheduled a series of public hearings to gather taxpayer input, to listen as John Q. Public vented, pro or con, on the subject of what to do with Niagara Falls' high schools.

Sensitive to the nature of the community, Granto slated forums city-wide to enable the greatest number of interested folks to participate. There were daytime sessions and evening sessions; meetings with PTA groups and service clubs and labor unions; presentations for minority organizations and editorial boards. Eighty-eight in all over a four-month period.

They met in school auditoriums and senior center cafeterias, executive conference rooms and church basements, any space that could accommodate. Each was fully documented and the collection remains preserved for posterity's sake in the lower bowels of the Board of Education annex.

The record will show that principal-on-special-assignment DiFrancesco even staged one session in the driveway of a concerned citizen. "They were worried about the potential for sewer back-ups," he explained. DiFrancesco listened to the residents' concerns and calmly explained why the project would not trigger their feared side-effect.

And so it went. Over a period of four months, Granto and Co. met with groups ranging in size from a handful to a roomful, staging the same presentation for each: Slide show, charts, Q&A, projections.

As expected, district officials were barraged with concerns, questions and, of course, criticisms. Residents questioned everything from the need to the very timing of the process. They worried about tax impact, about the effect upon the student population; they worried about the ramifications for adjoining business areas if the two existing high schools were to be closed.

They wondered about the impact on property values and the effect of an increased workload on an already aging infrastructure of roads, sewers and water lines.

Getting It Done

    In the end their concerns were heard and recorded, their questions answered as best possible. It was an eye-opening experience for all involved.

    The one true consensus to emerge from it all? A unanimous recognition that something tangible needed to be done, and soon. As the brutally candid DiFrancesco noted on more than one occasion, "we couldn't have gone two more years in that (old) building. Everything was breaking down terribly."

    Granto ultimately set a deadline of March 27, 1996, for his recommendation to the school board — then set out to hear as many opinions in the interim as possible.

    There was no shortage. Build at DeVeaux (a long-deserted satellite campus of nearby Niagara University, located on the edge of the lower Niagara River gorge). Consolidate at the LaSalle site. Just fix up what you have.

    It went on and on like that, over the course of several weeks. Lots of opinions, little consensus.

A VOICE OF REASON

    It was during a meeting at the 60th Street Elementary School that the pendulum begin to swing toward building new, at a site that had previously not been considered: A sizable parcel adjacent to the centrally located Hyde Park and its sprawling municipal golf course.

    Granto recalls vividly the moment when a regular Joe — city resident Joseph Nagelhout, to be exact — raised his hand and made the suggestion that the abandoned, overgrown plot would serve as an ideal "neutral site" for a new school.

    Nagelhout, with two children of his own attending city schools, explained later that as he listened to Granto's presentation, several questions ran through his mind. Does spending money on a 71-year-old building make the best business sense? Does building a new 800-student school make any more sense? Would consolidation at the 40-year-old LaSalle site — a facility said to be in line for major boiler and roof repairs within the next five years — be any more sensible?

    Nagelhout said he wondered how renovation to either site could occur without significant disruption of classes.

In his own mind, Nagelhout kicked around the options before realizing a simple fact: big business faces such decisions routinely and, inevitably, the choice is to consolidate, reduce overhead and save money.

So that became his suggestion to Granto. Combine two schools into one new building bordering Hyde Park. Sure, there would be substantial startup costs, but they would be offset by savings down the road.

To Nagelhout's credit, the proposed location was plenty large enough to accommodate a "super school" capable of housing the combined populations of both NFHS and LaSalle. And building there would entail absolutely no displacement of residents, no disruption to existing businesses. Another plus.

Just as importantly, it would not disturb the educational process; the existing buildings could remain open while construction commenced.

On the other hand, there were some serious questions pertaining to the site, which was bordered on the other sides by an industrial area and a public housing complex.

The most pressing: Was the area contaminated? And what of the deed to Hyde Park, which stipulated the land had to be used for recreational purposes?

Moreover, Granto wondered how potential development would impact those huge New York State Power Authority conduits, which ran diagonally beneath the parcel in question.

Considering all those factors, initially Nagelhout's idea "was greeted skeptically," Granto recalls. "Frankly, I figured the guy didn't know what he was talking about."

But that didn't stop him from investigating the site further.

"We all jumped in our cars after the meeting," DiFrancesco said. "I thought, 'Why didn't we think of this?' It gives us a campus with little disruption to the community, it's as central as can be, it offered an outlet for recreational activities. It was right there all the time."

"I literally can remember the winter day we drove out to the middle of the city because someone had suggested the site," recalls board member Mark Zito. "I felt from a business practicality standpoint it made sense — square in the middle of a shrinking city. It was shrinking from both ends, so we would meet in the middle."

Another advantage: The relative isolation of the site would indirectly serve to discourage class-cutting. Unlike the two existing schools, each located squarely in the heart of commercial districts, the Hyde Park site would place a new school in close proximity to virtually nothing attractive to teenagers — provided they were not golf enthusiasts. Even at that, the course is closed the vast majority of time that school is in session.

Oh, and for those students feeling they might need a little "divine intervention" come test time: the site was bordered on one edge by a quaint little Methodist church.

Another big check in the "plus" column.

Those conduits? Yes, they presented a problem. Their presence limited the "usefulness" of the plot, rendering a full 55 of the 65 total acres immune to excavation. Those 55 acres could support parking lots, or sporting fields, but not a massive building.

Still, 10 acres would be more than sufficient for the actual building, planners decided.

"The more we checked the site out, the better it looked," Granto said. "The moral is, you never know where your best advice will come from. That's a key talent: To take everything seriously, and give it a good listen."

"Everybody, including the board of education, agreed it was the best way to go," DiFrancesco said. "So (the SHEC team) went back to the drawing board" to formulate a proposal for "one central, modern, up-to-date facility."

The so-called "Hyde Park Site" was hastily added to the list of potential options being presented to the public. And from that day on — in Granto's mind, at least — it became the front-runner in the event a new school were to be built.

For his part, Nagelhout (ironically a former student of DiFrancesco's) received the district's Golden Apple Award, recognizing outstanding contributions to the school system, for his suggestion.

"We talk about him frequently," Granto says today.

Back then, however, the public forums continued, and the school board invested $80,000 to study the site's viability. And despite nearly constant questioning, Granto steadfastly refused to tip his hand, expressing no personal preference in the matter.

A TIP OF THE HAT

On Jan. 16, 1996, the setting was the Niagara Gazette conference room; the audience consisting of members of the newspaper's editorial board. Granto used the occasion to voice — for the first time publicly — his preference for erecting a new school.

In response to a question inquiring whether renovation of (or consolidation into) one of the existing buildings would result in an atmosphere as conducive to learning as an entirely new facility, Granto was quick to respond an emphatic "no."

"In my opinion, build new," he told the collection of reporters and editors assembled at the table. "Look at this in the long term as having a new school for the community of the future."

He was then asked of the prospective sites; does location make any difference in terms of the best education?

"I think it does in this sense," Granto said. "An area that is green and open will give (students) a totally different feel for learning." He continued on to say that the Hyde Park site under consideration offered "a unique opportunity to blend this area into one, to tie it in together."

So the stage had been set, the hand tipped ever so slightly.

The following day it was on to a meeting with the school district's Central Shared Decision-Making Committee. Over the course of the discussion, it became apparent that community sentiments were gradually changing in favor of a new school.

"You are better off building a new school, but I'd hate to see that old building close up," one concerned citizen told Granto. Another pointed out that a new facility would serve to increase property values, an issue of understandable concern among many residents.

Getting It Done

At a meeting with members of the Rotary Club the following week, the trend continued.

"You said if you (renovated) NFHS, you would still have to do LaSalle in five to 10 years," one concerned member pointed out. "Build a super school now to avoid the problems. Have two principals at the site and you would still have two separate schools."

That Rotarian may not have realized it at the time, but he said a mouthful in terms of how secondary education would look in Niagara Falls' future. *A super school that was actually two separate schools, with separate principals.* Intriguing.

Concerns were voiced over the community's ability to foot the bill for whatever project was determined best. "We used to be a city of 100,000 plus," one member noted. "As population decreases, has that been taken into consideration in computing indebtedness for the district and the people who will be here? Where will you get the money?"

"We try to maintain the tax levy," Granto responded. "We have to face who we are and what we are in determining what we are going to be." And what Niagara Falls was, was a shrinking city with a matching financial outlook.

Granto explained that district projections showed a continuing decline in population, from the current level of about 52,000 to a more likely 45,000 by the end of the 21st century's first decade.

There was one caveat, however.

"The number of students has not declined proportionately" to the general population decline, Granto pointed out. "We are looking at a low of 8,200 students." And with local private school enrollment already declining, he said, "we may get some of that population back if we offer a new school and new programs."

With the tone shifting toward a consensus for building new, the focus then turned toward location.

"Wouldn't it make more sense to put a high school in the center of the population?" a Rotarian asked.

Interest in the Hyde Park site seemed to grow from meeting to meeting. Sitting down with the District Parent Committee and the LaSalle Middle School PEG hours after the Rotary presentation, Granto was asked if the site were large enough to accommodate a "super school."

"Yes," he replied. "That was my recommendation given today at my forum at the Rotary — do it all at once." He reiterated the district's population projections for another concerned parent, adding "we must face the realities; maybe we are a one-high school city."

BIGGER SCHOOL, BIGGER PROBLEMS?

Concerns about sports teams and scholarship opportunities were aired, with one educator stating that "in one large high school, you would have fewer kids" having the opportunity to win scholarships for sports.

Reducing the chances for local kids to attend quality colleges via athletic scholarships didn't seem like an acceptable alternative. Even those not vying for scholarships would suffer, another reasoned, with fewer chances to participate in sports.

"We would be going into this gigantic high school," one concerned mother complained. "Would we have only one football team? One basketball team? My concern is, what is going to happen to the kid who may not be the best and is being carried? Can a district only keep one (team in each sport) or can you have two?"

It was just one of many concerns the district leadership had anticipated and brain stormed in advance.

"Our students are dwindling when it comes to sports," Granto explained. "But maybe we could have a bigger freshman team, or an active intramural program. We would have the resources to do it."

Cost was the primary concern when the scene shifted to a presentation for members of the Pine Avenue Business Association, the city's foremost business organization.

Questions were raised over the spiraling costs of previous projects, the maintenance costs for the existing high schools and the potential expense for a new building.

One member expressed a preference for a downsized renovation project, an initiative that would require special permission from the State Education Department to circumvent prescribed classroom size.

"You have to bring the building to code compliance," Granto replied. "Based on our past negotiations with the state, I know (the SED) will not consider a waiver on class size."

Besides, Granto reasoned, "Why shouldn't our students — your children — have an ideal program? You cannot take the short-term profit view of this. You have to take the long-term profit view. If our charge is to educate your children for the 21st century, there is a correlation between the atmosphere of the building they are in and their learning."

On April 25, 1996, Granto announced that he had ruled out building on north Main Street or the former mega-mall site on the city's east side — a decision that alleviated some of the pressure on his school board president.

"I'd had a lot of pressure from being involved on North Main Street for so many years," said Don King, whose downtown staple, The Wellesley Dress Shop, anchored the far end of Main Street for years.

Displacing too many homes — not businesses — turned out to be the major drawback for Main Street. The east side site simply had too many negatives attached.

Feeling he needed more information and more time to adequately evaluate the options, Granto pushed back his original deadline for a decision. When the time arrived, however, he was confident and decisive.

Following a compelling presentation which underscored the superintendent's very polished persuasive prowess, the Niagara Falls Board of Education on May 22, 1997 voted unanimously to build the new school at the Hyde Park site, using Minneapolis-based energy devices giant Honeywell Incorporated as the preferred developer.

In making his monumental recommendation during a public Board of Education meeting, Granto took the rather unusual first step of citing verse from the Bible:

"Where there is no vision, the people perish," he said, quoting from Proverbs 29:18. He told those in attendance that the passage reflected the dilemma facing Niagara Falls for a number of years already. The community had wandered aimlessly, holding no plan or vision for what it was or could be. By failing to plan, he told those in attendance, we were planning to fail.

Drawing upon the words of futurist Joel Barker, he continued: "Vision without action is merely dreaming," he said, "and action without vision is merely spinning wheels. But action combined with vision can change the world."

He went on to recommend that the district not only build new at the Hyde Park site, but also combine populations and close the existing two high schools.

"We knew that both economically and feasibly, we had to go to one facility," Granto explained. "And we knew we just couldn't convert the old high school for that (combined) facility. We just couldn't do it.

"LaSalle — it was not geographically feasible. It was in the middle of a very busy commercial strip, and we'd already had one fatal accident (involving a student pedestrian) there. I didn't want to put 2,500 kids there." So the Hyde Park site was the answer.

In the face of public apprehension, Granto cited recent precedence for such a bold move. Consolidation was successfully accomplished in 1992 in Schenectady, New York, where the Linton and Mount Pleasant schools merged into one. Assistant principal Rich Oleniczak — ironically, an NFHS grad — assured Falls administrators and school board members that the switch came off with few hitches. He reported some lingering resistance, particularly with longtime residents, but said it didn't stand in the way of a successful transition.

Three schools were merged into one in Utica, New York in 1987. Superintendent Tarasi Herbowy, while noting some resentment, told locals that oftentimes moves necessary for the betterment of students "are unpopular with taxpayers."

In his final word on the topic, Granto reminded his board that Trott students were seamlessly absorbed into the LSHS and NFHS populations when that building was closed in 1988. He also noted that a merger would mean a reduction in the duplication of services, resulting in financial savings and enabling greater program selections for students. And the two

Getting It Done

closed properties could be sold and returned to the tax rolls, providing the district some financial wherewithal.

Consolidation was the ticket, pure and simple. On Nov. 20, 1997, after considerable additional study to ascertain the ramifications of consolidating two high schools into one, the school board voted to build the new school for 2,500 students.

Niagara Falls was to become a one-high-school town. The only problem now: finding a way to pay for it.

CHAPTER 4
SHOW ME THE MONEY

How does the notorious Attica (New York) Correctional Facility — home to the bloodiest prison uprising in United States history — figure into the once-blurry picture that eventually focused as the new Niagara Falls High School? Glad you asked.

It was during a return trip from Albany some dozen years ago — another of the seemingly endless string of glad-handing excursions that lawmakers have come to expect and school administrators say reduces them to little more than professional panhandlers — that Granto's right-hand man, district business officer Roy Rogers, first heard on the radio about New York State's plan for selling the prison to private concerns, and then leasing the facility back at a substantial long-term cost savings.

That got Rogers to thinking. If it could work for the state, why not its school districts?

The more he and Granto kicked around the concept, the more sense it seemed to make. Then they added their own little twist to the equation: rather than wasting such a good idea on an existing facility — one for which the district had already laid out significant capital to erect and maintain — why not start from scratch? Build something truly historic — on someone else's dime, mind you — and then play rent-to-own.

Imagine it: a sparkling new school, built with private funds ... leased back at a fraction of that cost over a period of many years ... saving all that interest, all those maintenance costs ...

A revolutionary idea, to say the least. And one probably too good to ever come true. Niagara Falls was a poor district, after all, one of the poorest in the entire state. And this was a pipe dream of Cinderellan proportions.

Some time passed between the moment of that fateful news broadcast and the day Rogers received a phone call from the Buffalo Partnership, a local think-tank consisting of top business and civic leaders. The Partnership was seeking input

Getting It Done

on ways to improve that city's crumbling school stock via an infusion of private money.

That led to the head honchos of the Falls and Buffalo city school districts, along with top minds from the Buffalo Partnership, huddling up to formulate a plan. With critical input from the Partnership's Marshall Wingate and Buffalo Common Council member Arthur Eve, a rudimentary proposal was formulated to "privatize" public education. It would require the blessing of the state legislature, via special "enabling" legislation, and the Western New York contingent fully realized that gaining that support would be paramount to the success of the plan.

Around that same time, a somewhat similar privatization proposal had come out of New York City pertaining to the construction of a convention center there, although it did not require special legislative action. Even so, elements of that proposal were integrated into the Western New York school plans.

Now it was time to run it up the flag pole and see who saluted.

"Buffalo (school officials) approached the Western New York delegation" seeking a meeting in Albany, said Francine Delmonte, then chief of staff for Assemblyman Joseph Pillittere. "They made a pitch for doing (with Buffalo schools) what eventually happened in Niagara Falls."

Falls school officials were solidly on board, as well, hoping to be included in what surely would be a ground breaking legislative package.

"Our initial intention was to build Niagara Middle School" via privatization, Rogers said of the district's early 1990s plan to convert an abandoned, former all-girl Catholic high school into a state-of-the-art prep school.

Ultimately, the legislation failed and the Falls district achieved the $6 million Niagara Middle project via more conventional means.

That didn't stop district officials from pursuing that very attractive idea of privatizing school construction, however. Eventually it became clear that Buffalo would have to be dropped from the proposal in order to move it forward.

Mike Kurilovitch

NOTHING PERSONAL ...

"We were never going to get it through with Buffalo included," Rogers said. "The working agreement between the city and the (Buffalo) board of education wasn't so good at the time — now it has improved — so dropping Buffalo made the idea more politically acceptable in Albany. So later it became only a one-issue bill: just Niagara Falls."

Ultimately the issue became even more narrowly focused: Just Niagara Falls, and just ONE school.

Certain lawmakers viewed the pared-down proposal as a good pilot opportunity, a low-risk chance to see if privatization were, indeed, plausible.

The Falls proposal was completely reworked, Granto said.

"We didn't pattern it after anything. We made it up whole hog," he said. "Then we found out that it was all legal in New Jersey, but it was moot by then."

Game plan in hand, Falls officials set out to convince the state of the plan's merits ... the state legislature, that is, not to mention the state Education Department, state labor organizations ...

To do so would require sound strategy, reminiscent of that espoused by a tactical Bill Murray (portraying the tormented groundskeeper Carl) in the immortal golf classic "Caddyshack."

Eyeing up the pesky gopher believed responsible for turning the luxurious 36-hole Bushwood Country Club course into a 72-hole crater-fest — accomplished while effectively eluding Murray's many attempts at "elimination" — he comes up with a failsafe plan:

"My foe, my enemy, is an animal," he muses, calmly fashioning plastique explosives into a gopher look alike. "In order to conquer him I have to think like him and, whenever possible, to look like him," he concludes, contorting his face and plunging headlong into the heady world of the buck-toothed varmint.

To win state approval for the school construction plan meant the Falls delegation had to "think like the state." To do so entailed entering the STATE OF DOGGED DETERMINATION.

Geographically this might fall somewhere between New Jersey and New Jerusalem; philosophically it meant confronting a world in which political turf was just as doggedly defended, and incremental progress was gained only through gritty give-and-take, subtle negotiation and strategic concession.

The battle turned into a marathon not for the weak of stomach nor faint of heart, a political tug-of-war far outlasting a "real" war (the Persian Gulf skirmish with Saddam Hussein's Iraq), and with only minimally fewer casualties.

Granto and Rogers knew full well that the only way to be assured of getting the building they wanted would be to retain control of the construction process. To do so would require, in part, having final approval of all sub-contractors. The district would also protect its interests by establishing a team to oversee all aspects of the ongoing project, with weekly updates and troubleshooting sessions designed to head off problems and circumvent cost overruns.

It was all a part of the plan.

OPERATION PRIVATIZE
FRONT LINE: ALBANY

In the end, the biggest obstacles to erecting a shiny, new public school using very private dollars turned out to be the longstanding state laws clearly prohibiting such a venture, and the hardheaded politicos bent on enforcing them to the letter.

Well, that *and* finding investors willing to *put up* those private dollars. But first things first ...

Convincing those in elected office that privatization was the way to go for public school construction was akin to pushing term limits — as in *single* terms. It left a bad taste, particularly amongst those whose campaigns had ridden the backs (not to mention the pocketbooks) of organized labor.

After all, these infidels from Western New York were talking about *circumventing* the coveted Wicks Law, widely hailed as a fundamental safeguard for construction contractors.

How would that sit with constituents? And what would it translate into come election time?

Fortunately, by the time Granto and Co. returned to Albany to lobby for legislation permitting a new Niagara Falls High School, the privatization idea was no longer "new." The "radical" concept had been kicking around since the calendar was flipping over to 1990, and reluctant lawmakers had had some time to get accustomed to the prospect.

Imagine: a seemingly common-sense proposal that had been in the works since the *original* George Bush inhabited the White House (ironically building a coalition to support U.S. military strikes in the Middle East) and New York's now sad history of chronically late state budgets was still a relatively new phenomena ...

That is how long this idea had been in the pipeline, how long it had been caught up in the "talking" stage.

The time had come for action, and the Falls contingent was determined. The timing was right, the climate seemed right and the idea itself was simply too exciting to permit its defeat via sustained political foot dragging.

Local lawmakers John Daly (at the time in his final year in office) and Joseph Pillittere led the push in Albany, and school district officials chipped in by doing "a lot of lobbying," Rogers recalls.

Early progress came in increments best measured on a micrometer. Understandably, organized labor solidly opposed the concept.

"At one point," Pillittere said, "there was a problem with the plumbing contractors and the National Labor Board" with regards to eliminating the Wicks Law.

Ahh yes, the Wicks Law: a handy, labor-friendly little piece of legislation named for the late state legislator. Originally formulated to help combat corruption on public works projects, Wicks features three major components: it guarantees competitive bidding on public works projects; prescribes individual contractors for the four major project components (general, electrical, plumbing, and heating/air conditioning); and assures unions of earning the "prevailing wage" on any and all such projects.

Good for unions, good for contractors ... bad for school districts trying to shave peripheral costs in order to achieve "the most bang for the buck," as Granto would say.

The plumbers didn't relish the idea of being sub-contractors to a general contractor. "They felt the general contractor would squeeze the subs for profits," Rogers said.

"I wasn't overly pleased at first, to say the least," said Mike Redmond, then-business manager for the Plumbers and Steam fitters local. "For years (Wicks) had been the way business was done on public projects in New York State ... (but) there's no way that high school would have been built under traditional methods.

"(The school district) came to the Building Trades Council (of Niagara County), told us what they wanted to do and said 'We need your cooperation'," Redmond recalled. "They needed certain concessions that they knew were not good, politically, for the unions."

Abiding by the Wicks Law would have added another 10 to 15 percent in management and construction costs to the project, Granto said. That could have killed the project entirely, or at least put a major crimp on the grandeur planned. So the district had to find a way around the plumbers' concern

"The way we avoided that was having the school district sit in on all negotiations with the sub-contractors," Rogers said. "We established a set amount that resulted in some incentive for the general contractor, but with more benefit going to the school board than the general contractor."

Pillittere recalled that the original proposal forwarded by Niagara Falls also "didn't call for certain prevailing wages for unions." That presented a problem both for the plumbers and the NLRB.

Solution: a Project Labor Agreement with each of the contractors, guaranteeing the exclusive use of local union labor at prevailing wage. In return, the district would be permitted to circumvent the traditional bidding process, instead employing a negotiated contract with a single general contractor who would operate within a guaranteed maximum price.

"Since we had to pay prevailing wage anyway, that got us a lot of benefits," Granto explained. "Manpower levels were lowered, we got a no-strike clause, we eliminated 'rain days' (in which workers receive four hours pay for coming in, even if weather conditions preclude their working)."

"We were willing to trade off with the guarantee that the job would be all union labor," Redmond said. "We knew it would be the only way the school would get built. I took a beating from some fellow members downstate for the position I took," he said, "but we wouldn't have that school there now had we not come to this type agreement."

The deal was significant to both the district and to the various unions which would be involved in the project. The district would save money — lots of it, which could then be redirected back into the project — while the union received important assurances — not to mention copious work — for its members.

"We felt that these guys live in our city, pay taxes in our city and send their kids to our schools," Granto said. "Why shouldn't they get the work?"

By employing a "Request for Proposals" process rather than competitive bidding, the district was able to avoid "being locked in to low bids," Rogers said. "We were free to negotiate a price."

But why not go with low bidders?

"Low bid is a good process," Rogers explained, "but it doesn't always represent the best value."

A LOVE OF LABOR

The plumbers were by no means the only ones somewhat "apprehensive" over the initial plan.

"We had to deal with all different groups opposed to it, and for good reasons," Pillittere said. "There was concern about bypassing existing law, and that once we did it we would continue to do so. People felt we were destroying a law providing protection for different unions. So it was a real slow, drawn-out process."

"It was really historic in a couple of ways," said Senator George Maziarz of the protracted struggle. "We have never in the State of New York had a private developer build a school with this lease-back kind of arrangement. So that took special legislation.

"On top of that, there has never been (a Wicks Law) exemption in New York State. We did not want to go back to the days of historic corruption. Most of the labor unions love the Wicks Law and are very opposed to any kind of repeal."

A problem? You bet. But not an insurmountable one, as it turned out.

Eventually, "we had great support from local labor," Rogers said. "They actually lobbied with us and for us to get that exemption. It took numerous meetings with labor councils, their local Albany lobbyists and the Chamber of Commerce to get that support."

But get it they did.

Next up: the State Education Department.

"We had to get the State Education Department on board, and convince them this was a good thing," Maziarz recalled. "We said, let's try it, and if it works we can use it in other parts of the state. We presented it as a pilot program; maybe if we did something outside the norm, it could be something the rest of the state would look at — if it were successful.

"It really was a gamble. We needed the governor and the legislature and the State Ed Department on board."

Daly, Pillittere and crew — buoyed by Granto's success with the local unions — began to feverishly work the legislative end.

Maziarz's office, meanwhile, took up the battle on the national labor front. His Albany chief of staff, Laurie Pferr (who previously held a similar post in Daly's office), did much of the behind-the-scenes maneuvering with State Ed, while also tap-dancing with the Majority Leader's office, the Assembly, the Speaker, the program and finance people ...

"George worked directly with the unions, while I worked with some lobbyists representing some of the larger national labor unions," Pferr said. "They were nervous. They were strongly opposed. They felt it was very precedent-setting," and it wasn't necessarily the type of precedent they wanted set.

"It took a very integrated effort to build support with labor," Pferr said. Assurances were given that the project would utilize local labor, a major concession on the part of project organizers.

Back at the Capital, Pillittere ran into opposition from the state comptroller's office.

"I convinced the comptroller that ... the district was not building the school," Pillittere recalls. "It was being built by a private contractor with a guarantee that the district would rent it back for a specified period of time. That took it out of the realm of state law. In a way It's still a public school, it's just not publicly built. That was something completely new, a brand-new concept. Something that's not been done in New York State before. It was a time-consuming event that I had to carry the ball for. I thought the concept was great."

The State Education Department, said Maziarz, was "skeptical at first. It was really out of the norm for them."

Once State Ed finally opted in, it was time to wrap up the legislative end of the equation.

WITH A LITTLE HELP FROM MY FRIENDS

"It was a matter of me convincing the governor (by this time, Pataki) that this was not an attack on union labor and that it would ultimately be a good thing — a pilot that might revolutionize the way we build school buildings," Maziarz said. "It took some major convincing."

With support mounting, time eventually became the primary villain.

"It didn't get through the Legislature until very late in the session," Maziarz said. "A lot of people were skeptical. They aren't keen on doing things differently."

With Pillittere (who gained stature with his first-of-its-kind environmental work regarding the Love Canal disaster and subsequent Right-To-Know legislation) working the Assembly side and Maziarz the Senate, legislators started falling into line. By the time it came to a vote, "it passed strongly," Maziarz said. "There were just a couple negative votes."

The Assembly needed a little more convincing.

"I remember adjourning at 6 a.m.," Pillittere said. "It was a real last-minute session. At 1:15 in the morning they wanted a late amendment. Maziarz was fantastic with his involvement. It finally passed somewhere around 5:30 or 6 in the morning on the last day of our session.

"It was something that hadn't been tried before, but it worked out great. The school district and the residents of Niagara Falls saved money. It worked out that everyone saved money."

Governor George Pataki signed the legislation into law on Aug. 8, 1996, officially setting the Niagara Falls City School District on course to erect the nation's premier high school.

Passage of the enabling legislation was tremendously satisfying — although not totally expected, Maziarz admitted.

"I thought quite frankly when we started that it would be 50-50 at best," he said. "Once the unions came on board, that was a major piece. And that was pretty much due to the efforts of Carmen Granto and (Falls school board member and labor union representative) Mark Zito."

"It's really a very interesting little piece of legislation," Delmonte said. "It isn't a blanket law; it was drawn solely for Niagara Falls, so in that regard it's really very special. I'm very proud of that bill.

"It's a fairly complex bill. What we wanted to achieve had never been consummated in law, even in that New York City case. That was more administrative in nature."

"The novelty of it was intriguing," Delmonte continued. "The Niagara Falls City School District wanted to build a super high school. We looked at it solely from a legislative standpoint — not from the perspective of combining schools, or of its potential impact on the community. We didn't know at the time what the legislation would spawn. This was nuts-and-bolts stuff, and it was up to the school district to determine how it would all come together — the combining, the closing. How it was to turn out was something completely separate from the legislative end.

"It did create some conflict within the community, on location and the combining of schools and such. But aside from that, it went well, and it was something to be proud of, that we were able to pull it off. We treaded into unknown waters, and it was nice to make that kind of history.

"It was a tough sell, believe me. The Assembly is very cautious in these types of ventures. It did not pass without a lot of thought, consideration and study work."

One of the leading opponents had been Steve Sanders (D-Manhattan), then-chairman of the Assembly Education Committee.

"He really was very resistant," Delmonte said. "Joe (Pillittere) almost came to physical blows with him towards the end of the session. He really gave it some heavy-duty scrutiny."

"Sanders hated the bill," Pillittere recalled. "He was chairman of the (education) committee, and his responsibility was to determine whether the legislation was good or bad. He totally disliked it because there were just too many changes" from standard operating procedure for his taste.

"I had to get the bill out of his committee, and he wouldn't let it out. One time in the Speaker's office area I had some really nasty words with him," Pillittere said. "It gets frustrating, especially when you've been working 18 hours and you haven't had anything to eat all day, and you're just waiting for the bill to be approved so you can get it on the floor. Tempers can get a little raw.

"I didn't want to wait until the last minute for fear I wouldn't get the bill. In my 20 years in office that was the most difficult bill I had to get passed through the Assembly. It took probably 85 percent of my energy for that whole (legislative session). I had to talk to every committee member, the speaker, many different people. I had to give up a lot to get that bill out. It was definitely not my most relaxing year in office."

Said DelMonte: "In the end, the difference was that the school district had covered a lot of bases. They had brought the unions on board with it. That was a good couple years of work for them, but it helped pave the way. Quite frankly, if the unions had been opposed, it would have been a much tougher haul. The school district did its homework and came prepared. And Joe went through all the travails (with them). Joe had always taken the lead in the Assembly. He was the one consistent force.

Getting It Done

"People don't realize sometimes to what extent you have to go to make these things happen. It takes time. It takes a lot of time. It wasn't willy-nilly, not this bill."

"To (Niagara Falls') credit, they did a good job in putting it all together," Delmonte said. "It worked well, and it very well could be a model for future school construction."

For those who had been through the mill with the idea, seeing it finally come to fruition was a cathartic experience.

"As each hurdle passed, reality became more and more apparent," Rogers said. "It was really kind of amazing. You don't realize what you have done until you see the building and realize it went from idea to reality.

MEANWHILE, BACK AT THE FARM ...
FRONT LINE: NIAGARA FALLS

All of the wrangling, all the negotiation, all the political give-and-take in Albany and beyond ... it had "Waterloo" written all over it, but the "bulldog" bit down and persevered. It was a monumental victory, to be sure, yet just another battle in an ongoing war.

Back home, a united uprising threatened to quash the budding school project again, long before the first shovel ever hit the ground.

Surveying the battleground, Granto's resolve was bolstered by a little historical introspection.

"The first blow is half the battle," wrote Oliver Goldsmith in "She Stoops to Conquer" (1773). Granto knew it, and he knew the first, and perhaps biggest blow, had already been struck. Some disgruntled neighbors couldn't be allowed to stand in the way, not after all that had already transpired ...

Granto's long awaited, close-the-existing-schools-and-merge-into-a-new-building announcement had met with the expected reaction locally, a mixed bag of cheers and jeers.

Despite the fact that a decision had finally been reached, those resilient NIMBY's were not about to go away quietly.

In July 1997, Porter Road area residents organized in their opposition to the proposed school, saying it would disrupt their quiet residential neighborhood. Hundreds of people signed a petition asking the City Council to vote down a proposed lease for the school site.

Group members cited concerns for student safety, saying that nearby high-tension wires represented a health concern — not to mention a growing landfill (sarcastically dubbed the "Mount CECOS Ski Resort" by local punsters) located less than a mile away.

They expressed apprehension over traffic — especially buses — saying increased travel would necessitate road-widening, lead to additional hazards and, ultimately, reduce neighborhood property values.

They questioned how the project would impact area wildlife populations and worried that the city's fire department was ill-equipped to respond to any potential fires in a four-story super structure such as the new high school.

Sewer and water lines represented another potential problem area.

City Council members shared many of the concerns, especially over the viability of Porter Road for handling upwards of 40 buses on a twice-daily basis. The school district was required to perform extensive traffic studies on all roads which would be affected by the project.

Granto himself launched the damage-control campaign, pointing out to those worried about "trespassing walkers" that no one would be walking through the neighborhood who didn't already live there. Of the roughly 2,500 students expected to attend the new school, only 335 would be walkers, down from 800 at the district's two existing schools. The remainder would be bused, drive themselves or be dropped off by parents.

As far as concerns over the park deed, Granto emphasized to City Council members that no park land was being considered for the project. The parcel in question lies adjacent to park, he told them, *bordering* but not infringing upon golf course (hence, park) property.

No infringement upon park lands equals no threat to park deed.

Sensing the potential for a political or court-imposed blockade, Granto wisely developed a contingency plan: if the city were to fail to come through with a lease for the Hyde Park

Getting It Done

lands, he recommended leasing the DeVeaux property from Niagara University and building a new school there.

It might even prove a better choice in the long run, what with that pastoral campus and picture-postcard gorge view. No wires, no landfills; only disgruntled potential neighbors, high costs and a bear of a daily bus ride for just about every kid attending.

Fortunately, it did not come down to that.

Environmental impact studies subsequently supported the district's contentions that the high-tension wires and landfill were negligible health risks. Likewise, building on the parcel in question would have no deleterious effect on area wildlife.

To appease resident concerns, district officials promised that bus traffic would be routed away from Portage Road. By adding a service road to the south end of the project, buses could be directed down Pine Avenue to a rear entrance to the school, a much more tenable proposition for all concerned, as it turned out.

Finally, in August, 1997, the district reached agreement with the Niagara Falls City Council on a lease for the designated site. The perfunctory $1 price initially discussed had ballooned to some $600,000, but the monetary aspect seemed almost irrelevant.

The agreement also called for the school district to accept responsibility for certain improvements to the adjacent community: drainage enhancements, particularly for the adjacent golf course; new sidewalks along Porter Road; and improvements to existing recreational facilities for both school and community use.

At long last the final piece was in place — even the Power Authority had released its interest in the land — allowing the project to move into its final stages.

Another blow struck, another step closer to victory …

BUT YOU STILL HAVEN'T SHOWN ME THE MONEY

In true Granto fashion — never leaving even the smallest detail to chance — the issue of funding the new school had been addressed in great detail long before a developer was ever named.

Not that funding was a minor detail, mind you; after all, we're talking of upwards of $100 million here. With that kind of money, there could be no t's left uncrossed, no i's undotted.

On April 16, 1998, the school board approved a $71 million contract with the Honeywell Corp. of Minneapolis. The 8-0 vote named the Honeywell firm as program manager, overseeing financing, planning and construction.

The "program manager" designation allowed the firm significantly greater input than a mere "construction manager," permitting the company's contribution in the design, schematic and construction phases, as well as the critical financing component.

Such a "value-added concept" of program management was made much easier with the critical Wicks Law exemption and the enabling legislation.

Honeywell subsequently tapped the J.P. Morgan company of New York City to attract investors willing to finance a piece of the $71 million construction. Certificates of Participation were sold, with these "speculators" to receive their return via the annual lease-back payments made by the district.

"The arrangement is similar to bonds, but they're actually buying a piece of each lease payment," Rogers said. "It amounted to tax-exempt financing. The project really wasn't feasible without it. That was a major hurdle."

This is where things start to get a little bit tricky.

Although Honeywell would essentially finance and erect the building — leasing it back to the district over a 30-year period — it would not actually *own* the facility.

School district attorney Angelo Massaro, seeking to protect the district's long-term interests, suggested creation of a special purpose entity group to "hold" the school property over the 30-year life of the lease.

The funding entity would receive annual payments of $5 million over the 30-year life of the lease.

So how does a "poor" district afford that arrangement? Well, like this: via State Education Department construction aid, a full 83 percent of the district's principal and interest costs would be reimbursable. The remaining 17 percent would be footed by the school district, but its obligation would be met without raising the tax levy. How? By using the savings realized from reduced operating costs (running one energy efficient school as opposed to two obsolete buildings), as well as other "performance contracts and value engineering," Massaro said.

The rather minuscule (proportionately, anyway) remainder would be covered by the profits realized from sale of the two existing buildings, as well as a $7 million contribution from the New York State Power Authority.

So that's how you get a brand-spanking new, state-of-the-art school without having to dig into your own pockets.

And that's how the money end of the lease works. Of course there are other ends, as well, and Massaro wanted to be certain none of them were loose enough to trip-up the district down the road.

"One of my biggest concerns," he explained, "was that we had to have a lease" addressing what happened at the end of that 30-year period "when your only high school is owned by an entity and still has 20 to 30 years of useful life left."

Loose end. Potential down side. Solution necessary.

"We had to consider all the variables 20 to 30 years down the road," Massaro said. "As it evolved, at the end of the 30 years the property reverts over to the district. It bonds over, the lease dissolves."

Lease paid off, district takes ownership, everyone walks away happy.

"That was a very significant thing," Massaro said. "Even today, people don't realize that Honeywell doesn't own that building. They (were) the project manager of it. So that was a very unique legal structure, again very significant because it overcomes the hurdle of 'what happens after 30 years'?"

"This was all rather remarkable when you were living through it," he said later.

That $7 million from the Power Authority? Glad you asked.

In an effort to be a good neighbor (it's 50-year federal license is rapidly approaching time for renewal, and stipulations therein require certain improvements to its home community), the Power Authority agreed to the contribution, providing it was not used for actual building construction. The donation was subsequently stipulated for use in the construction of various sporting and recreational facilities on the school campus.

"We knew it was an opportune time due to the relicensing," Granto said. "They needed to look like good guys and it was in line with their current license to improve recreational opportunities for the community. So we met with Power Authority staff and lawyers and made our pitch."

Granto recalls it as one of his finer moments.

"I was in a zone," he said. Gathered around a conference table in a "glitzy room," Granto reached back for one of his many old-time sports analogies.

"After we showed them the brochures and the numbers, I said 'Gentlemen, it's the bottom of the ninth, it's four to one and the bases are loaded. The count is three-and-two and there's two outs. No, do you want to be known as Ralph Branca or Bobby Thompson? You can really hit a home run with this one."

The district had sought $14 million; Granto's histrionics earned them $7 mill.

So in the final tally, it was $71 million in bonds, $5 million from the LaSalle sale, and $7 million from NYSPA.

Eighty-three million semolians. That can buy a whole lot of school.

Even so, it wasn't enough to do everything Granto had hoped. With $4 million needed to rebuild the stadium and another $1 million earmarked for sports facilities on the school campus, there wasn't enough left to cover the outdoor municipal pool at Hyde Park and make it into a year-round facility which could then be used by the schools.

So a pool was returned to the school drawings and the remainder of the Power Authority money was set aside for improvements at the Hyde Park Ice Pavilion.

The future of Niagara Falls was back on track.

"This is one of the biggest projects that has happened here in 30 years," Granto acknowledged. "We will have one high school for the 21st century for students who deserve nothing but the best."

Getting It Done

But city residents still wanted to know what the final cost to the district (read: themselves) would be from all this finagling.

Well, get your pencils and pads ready ...

After factoring in state reimbursement and debt service, along with the estimated $1 million annual savings from closing the two old schools ... then taking into account the district's $600,000 cost for the 99-year lease to the Hyde Park property ... as well as the agreed-to improvements and maintenance of Hyde Park facilities ... the total (annual) local share will be about $700,000.

The culmination of all "preliminaries" prompted another Granto sports analogy: "We're approaching the finish line and (the district) is riding Secretariat!"

Now that the hard part was over, Granto was asked, what's next?

"This was the easy part," he dead panned in response. "Trust me — the hard part will be coming up with a name."

CHAPTER 5
LINING UP KEY PLAYERS

The Honeywell Corp. first became associated with the Niagara Falls School District in 1996, when the firm was hired to perform energy retrofit operations on the district's 18 school buildings.

It's a popular program that Honeywell has instituted from coast to coast, including jobs done at some of the country's top sports arenas, city halls and even major military complexes. It works like this: Honeywell representatives study how much a customer pays for utilities — water, heat, hot water, air conditioning — then pledge to significantly lower those costs by replacing inefficient lights, boilers, air conditioning units, windows, water systems, control devices (valves, thermostats) and the like with more modern, energy-efficient models.

What makes it so attractive — at least in the case of Niagara Falls schools — is that the company guarantees its customers a percentage savings on its utility bills, with customer paying for the equipment retrofit from that savings.

If savings don't meet expectations, Honeywell makes up the difference. Exceeding expectations means the customer keeps the difference.

It's called performance-based contracting, and it's hard to say no to an arrangement like that.

Niagara Falls expected to save 30 percent, or $1.9 million in net energy costs, over the course of a decade.

Having partnered with the school district for so long, Honeywell was familiar with the ongoing drama over building a new school, and recognized the project as a unique win-win opportunity.

Eventually, that is.

When first approached by the district, Honeywell officials turned down the chance to be project developer, reasoning that they didn't want to get into the construction business.

High risk, low profit margins, they said. Too many things can go wrong.

Getting It Done

But the district persisted, and after a third request Honeywell finally reconsidered. Spokeswoman Kaye Veazay spoke to her company's interest in the project.

"It was appealing to Honeywell because the Niagara Falls School District was a good customer of ours, so it gave us an opportunity to strengthen our customer relationship.

"It also gave us an opportunity to showcase some of the most technologically advanced products we have to offer school systems."

Since showcase=exposure=business potential, Honeywell wanted in. Obtaining that "in" entailed a lengthy process.

At its meeting of Aug. 22, 1996, school board members discussed publicly, for the first time, the district's innovative plan to "lease-back" rather than own any new building.

Rogers, chief business administrator for the district, told board members that turning to a private developer to build the new school would be advantageous on several fronts. As planned, it would permit the district to bond costs over a 30-year period, as opposed to the traditional 10; would allow industry professionals to oversee construction, rather than district representatives ("we're in the business of teaching, not building" Granto likes to say); and would circumvent state requirements calling for four separate contractors on public projects — a move district officials at the time estimated could save from 13 to 20 percent on project costs.

In addition, the developer would be responsible for repairs and maintenance over the course of the lease, not the district, creating additional savings.

As originally proposed in sample legislation formulated by the district, the developer would own the building, but the district would retain rights to the property it sat upon, giving the district critical leverage in lease negotiations.

It was a ground breaking proposal, Rogers noted, and board members eagerly voted to send it on to the State Education Department, where it would receive close inspection over the next two months.

Ultimately, of course, the ownership issue evolved and Honeywell was, indeed, selected as project developer, in April, 1998.

Mike Kurilovitch

THE RIGHT MAN FOR THE JOB

"(Honeywell) had never done one of these before," said Steve Rollins. "They realized that now they had to deliver, and that's why they found me."

"I'd had all kinds of experience with projects of this type with other companies," Rollins said, including a stint as vice president of the largest construction management firm in the country. "I was recruited (by Honeywell) for this very kind of thing."

Rollins enjoyed a unique role within the Honeywell company, being named project executive for the Niagara Falls High venture. His assignment was overseeing this project and this project only.

"This was a first-of-its-kind venture for Honeywell," Rollins explained, and the company wanted a capable individual in place, to assure a successful outcome.

Rollins was already familiar with the Western New York area, having coordinated for his prior management firm the nearly $250-million modernization of the Roswell Park Cancer Institute in Buffalo.

At the conclusion of that project he was asked to relocate to Boston, but refused because his 6-year-old daughter "had fallen in love with Western New York." The Honeywell offer allowed him to stay in the area, so he accepted — despite the fact that the NFHS project "was actually a small project for me."

"I hadn't been physically out in the field managing one of these in 10 years, maybe longer," Rollins said, "so it was kind of stepping back in time."

From Rollins' perspective, most elements of the project were unremarkable: "You have an architect, a contractor, a construction manager and away you go," he said.

The financing part of it, that was unique. And it presented some unique challenges and benefits.

"It allowed us to have more of a quality-control situation with the procurement process," he said. "The contractors and sub-contractors. With circumvention of the Wicks Law, we had a chance to pre-screen the qualifications of bidders.

Getting It Done

"When you have public bids you put the bids out and that is the only shot you have. There's no opportunity to put limitations on the contractors who can bid. Anyone with $100 can pick up the documents, and on bid day the low bidder gets the project. (Screening) eliminates a lot of the potential for things to go wrong, such as someone going broke mid-job because they're over-extended.

"It filters out a lot of the contractors out there when you can actually do page-by-page review of bids. You can make sure they understand the scope of the project; it eliminates the possibility that a set of job specs might be overlooked, so you can go into the project knowing they have it all covered."

According to Rollins, "the public bid process (puts) some rather severe limitations on procurement, quite frankly. Outside it, you have the opportunity to develop a bid strategy. You can break out more things as separate contracts," such as roofing and structural steel.

"That's another quality-control process," Rollins said. "Plus it stimulates more competition. It allows contractors to specialize more, to focus on their unique strengths. It eliminates the need for subbing out."

It results in a better project, and it was all made possible by the privatization legislation.

"And I believe if it were properly replicated — the same as this project — you'd see more of this type of legislation," Rollins said. "How could you not? Building without raising the tax rate one cent?!"

Rollins noted the initial apprehension, particularly on the part of the plumbers, but said that their attitudes changed "180 degrees" when they saw how the project came down.

"They saw all the benefits," he said, "and they saw that all the things they were afraid of never materialized. Getting people who have done business the same way for 50 years to see things differently is always difficult," he said, "but it was nothing but good news" with the NFHS project.

The good news didn't come without one final bit of bad, however. One final hurdle — and a 10-foot-high one, at that.

Mike Kurilovitch

A BOLT FROM THE BLUE

In late June, 1997, the Board of Education got its first look at plans for the new building, which featured four, four-floor academic "towers," a concept that permitted the greatest flexibility for reconfiguration. The 419,000 square foot building would have been slightly smaller than the two former schools combined (448,000 square feet).

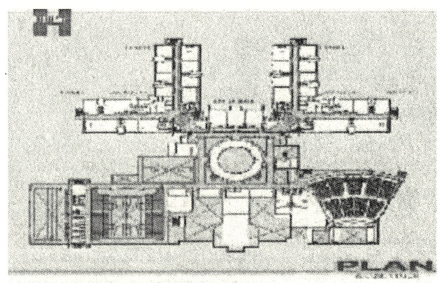

A view of the architectural plans for the second floor of the "new" Niagara Falls High School

Construction had been set to begin in September, 1997, already delayed nearly two months by difficulties encountered in the "coordination of all the key players," DiFrancesco said.

Part of the problem involved city department heads seemingly intent on disrupting the process.

"They're good people but they were not quite ready to move at the pace we were ready to," Granto said. "Mayor (James) Galie was very supportive ... it was just the system. I can see why developers don't want to work in the city. It's the attitude.

Getting It Done

Instead of working with you and helping you, it was like 'gotcha!' Like their job is to get you."

Granto illustrated his point with a tale of a seemingly pointless dispute over the type of drain pipe being used.

"We had two clashing cultures," Granto continued. "One was there with a vision and a mission to get it done. One was not quite sure why they were there.

"We had a lot to do just to make sure our guys didn't get discouraged by it. I can't remember one incident in which (city representatives) were prepared."

Further delays — this time on the part of the architects — prompted Granto to approach Rollins about taking over stewardship of the critical CORE Team meetings.

CORE was the forum the district had created for reviewing project progress and problems, impending changes, deadlines and the like. Key district staffers — from principals to maintenance crew and even teachers and students — the "end users" as Granto called them — met weekly with the project manager, architect and any other pertinent players.

"That was a key group," Granto said. "They met every week from preconstruction and planning, right through actual construction. (Rollins) said that group is what made the project come in on time and on budget. Having school personnel on-site at all times, things went from idea and change to change-order within minutes."

"We had to have a decision-making process that was good, one with checks and balances yet was timely," Granto said. "Time is money when you're in construction, and the board gave (CORE) the authority" to act as the district's watchdogs in the proceedings.

"Every person had responsibility. They went over the (project's) status every week, which helped us establish an esprit de corps. That was important," Granto said. "They were like the Marines — assess, adapt, adjust and overcome. If that wasn't their motto it was certainly their modus operandi."

Good thing, too, considering they presided over $5.8 million worth of change orders. But that's getting away from the point.

Rollins' assumption of the stewardship role turned out to be a pivotal move.

Mike Kurilovitch

TROUBLE IN PARADISE

"When I reviewed all the previous CORE Team minutes I saw a history of no closure," Rollins said. "Item after item. I do a task log when I need closing, when delivery deadlines are approaching. That lack of decisive leadership was letting issues go on and on and on. That's why they couldn't get things done."

Closer inspection revealed the project to be mired in some $9 million in cost overruns; to continue on at that rate would have spelled certain doom, as the August, 1998 sunset clause on the enabling legislation would have come and gone without so much as a shovel in the ground.

Rollins urged Granto to move quickly and decisively. Despite having had a good relationship with Stieglitz, Stieglitz and Mach, PC, in the past — the Niagara Middle School project being the primary example — the NFHS project, with all its intricacies and deadlines, was proving too much for the small architectural firm to handle.

At one point Stieglitz even merged with a Watertown, New York firm in a last-ditch maneuver to try to salvage its involvement in the project. The move came at the technical drawing stage — the time of conception, not of actual design — but the point of no return was quickly approaching. Unfortunately, squabbling and internal strife resulted in setbacks that further delayed progress.

The decision was made to replace the company after its lead designers left the firm mid-stream.

Rogers recalled the 1997 winter holiday period as particularly stressful for district officials. The decision to change architects at this stage of the game would clearly be make-or-break for the project; one false move now and the entire process would be down the drain, all those long months and years of planning, lobbying and hard work going for naught.

Despite the fact that the district literally had no other choice, cutting Stieglitz loose was still a difficult task.

"We'd had a good relationship with Stieglitz in the past," Rogers said. "They built our Niagara Middle School and did a tremendous job. They have good, imaginative people, but the firm was just too small for this project."

"They were just not as far along as they should have been," Rogers said, pausing briefly before adding, "but it really turned out to be a blessing. We made the decision to change architects between December 1997 and January 1998. We needed a large firm that could sink a lot of people into the project because we were running up against the sunset clause on the legislation. The law would have (expired) if there were not shovels in the ground soon."

CHAPTER 6
BACK TO THE DRAWING BOARD

Winter 1997 was at Niagara's doorstep when the cold reality of it all set in. Already behind schedule and with that sunset clause looming ominously, like a thunderhead on the horizon, the school district was once again forced to go knocking on the doors of prospective designers.

Time was of the essence now. The successful firm would have to condense its work into a time and space that would make Reader's Digest envious. Only firms of sufficient repute, vision and — most importantly — manpower, would be seriously considered for the monumental task which lay ahead.

Christmas lurked right around the corner when the search branched off to Princeton, New Jersey, headquarters for the award-winning Hillier Group. The world's third-largest architectural firm specialized in the design of school buildings and, as such, was somewhat familiar with the Niagara Falls project — although perhaps not quite in the way Falls officials would have preferred.

"We do large school projects so we had heard about it through the grapevine, basically," David Chase, principal-in-charge for The Hillier Group, said of the NFHS project. "We knew about the (legal) variances and so on. It was also kind of known in the (architectural) world that there were problems with the project."

Of course, since as early as Lucius Annaeus Seneca in the first century A.D., men have relished such challenge ...

"Fire is the test of gold," Seneca wrote, "adversity, of strong men."

Chase was clearly intrigued by the project.

Talks commenced, and the Falls contingent was impressed to learn that Hillier had, in fact, freshly completed a similarly ambitious project in East Orange, New Jersey, a project likewise relying upon "creative financing."

Talk about going to the head of the class? Hillier instantly shot to the top of Niagara's list.

With the calendar all but precluding a lengthy search process, Rollins figured it was high time to check in with his opinion on the subject.

"I'd had past experience with (Hillier) and knew that they had the horsepower to deliver," he said in making his preference clearly known to the district.

Coming from the guy who had diagnosed the design maladies in the first place, the recommendation gained instant favor amongst school officials. With their prospects for a happy new year hinging squarely upon the timely identification of a capable design team, district representatives immediately set out to achieve that objective. Destination: The Garden State.

"When we first interviewed we were told they wanted us to think outside the box, despite the limited time," recalled Jorge Luaces, studio principal and head designer for Hillier's K-12 studio. "It was a major challenge."

"We are a firm that thinks out of the box anyway," Luaces said, "and the board of education and the superintendent were able to see that. We want to move education forward, to give kids something more than just brick walls and an intimidating setting. We try for more of a college setting, something in which you can feel more free, more like human beings. We're not afraid to take risks."

It was that distinctive, forward-thinking and non-traditional approach that impressed Falls officials sufficiently for them to offer Hillier the contract.

Under the rather difficult circumstances presented, however, it was Hillier officials who had to do some serious soul-searching before the deal could be consummated.

"We knew we would have a very tight, difficult schedule to meet," Luaces said. "What usually takes 18 months was being compressed into six."

Could it be done? Would quality be sacrificed? Would the Hillier team — the Hillier company itself — be up to the laborious strain of delivering a quality product under such trying circumstances?

And just as importantly, what of the team on the other side of the drawing board? Any problems on the client's end—disagreement amongst board members, dissatisfaction with design elements — would only bog down the process and be magnified by the time constraints.

Was the district up to the task at hand?

Through hours upon hours of talks, the answer to that question became equally clear. The professionalism and level of commitment exhibited by Niagara Falls school officials— not to mention the incredible visibility afforded Hillier by involvement in such a high-profile project — ultimately persuaded the company's brain trust to sign on.

MAKING DIFFICULT DECISIONS EASIER

Luaces knew the project would be as demanding as any he had ever undertaken. But he also knew that taking it was the right choice.

"What helped was that the clients knew exactly where they were going," Luaces said. "They really understood what the process was like. They had assembled a superb, superb team of people to see this project through to fruition.

"The district was very smart in getting a great team together — Steve Rollins (from Honeywell) was a superb professional, Carmen Granto was a superb leader, and the Board of Education was very much united, unlike a lot of other boards. That makes life for us a lot easier. It was just a fabulous, fabulous experience for all of us."

The architectural snafu had cost the district precious months of project time, which would ultimately prove costly in the end. But in the final analysis it was merely another in a series of major hurdles which had to be cleared.

Granted, the bar had been brushed a tad this time — maybe even teetered a bit — but it never tumbled. And with Hillier joining the party, the project would very quickly be righted and set back on course.

ONLY THE BEGINNING ...

Locking up Hillier was the first step in correcting the course of the wayward project. Just how quickly it was righted, however, impressed even the likes of Chase.

"We presented a proposal to meet the project requirements regarding the sunset clause, as well as staying on budget. It was a total redesign, from zero — a completely different project," Chase pointed out.

Incorporating the best aspects of the original design with a new focus on more efficient use of space, Hillier architects came up with a sleeker, slightly scaled-down plan.

The four academic "towers" from the original plan were retained, but in "L-shaped" pairs. The redesign created a park-like courtyard facing the golf course.

While the courtyard was a nice "bonus," the tower redesign also carried with it several practical advantages. For starters, it reduced the total square footage of the project, rendering it more compact and efficient, a prime consideration due to the fact that construction was possible over only 10 of the 79 acres set aside for the campus.

Because of those hydroelectric conduits running beneath the property, much of the land had to be set aside and preserved, potential uses limited to such amenities as parking lots and sporting fields — uses that would require no digging or disruption to the earth — but little else. The conduits dictated exactly where construction could take place, and there was no negotiation possible.

The dog-leg tower design offered other benefits: it conserved space, improved heating/cooling efficiency and enhanced traffic flow.

There was a security concern as well, and the dogleg design answered it perfectly. By shifting the "houses" to one side of the building, the school could seal off the classroom areas while permitting maximum use of the remainder of the building — the auditorium and the sporting facilities — for after-hours activities.

While reducing the amount of space dedicated to hallways and stairways, architects nonetheless believed the new design to be more "user-friendly" in terms of traffic flow.

Needless to say, a lot of benefits were realized simply from the Hillier redesign.

Said Rollins: "What (Hillier) did for this project was nothing short of phenomenal. They took 420,000 gross square feet worth of drawings — 56 classrooms. They came on board and basically started from scratch. They felt the original design was too inefficient, that it didn't respond to the program. In five and-a-half months they delivered the documents. That's just unheard of.

"They reduced the square footage to 380,000 while increasing the number of classrooms from 56 to 71. They increased the designed occupational use of the building from 2,500 to 3,500. They did it by efficiency — square foot efficiency. You trim the corridors, the storage rooms, all those wasted spaces that don't count as usable square footage. That's how architectural firms are judged, by how efficient they can make a building. Hillier made the building more efficient."

Hillier's improvements were more than aesthetic, more than simply functional. They were revenue-generating.

"That allowed the district to realize more State Ed (department) money — they got the district a ton more money from the SED," Rollins said. "Of course, the more money SED comes up with, the more debt service (the school district) can afford — the more building they could afford to build."

Hillier's performance, in a word, was simply "extraordinary," said Rogers.

The biggest changes Hillier made involved relocating the library/media center to the center of the building, and the main parking lot from the south to the north side of the structure. The south side was now to be reserved strictly for bus traffic, so it could be segregated from cars and significantly decrease congestion.

Another integral change came about courtesy of the general contractors, the Ciminelli Construction Company of Buffalo, New York.

As Ciminelli chief operating officer John Giardino tells it, company officials recognized right off that the original all-brick design would not be feasible within the new construction timetable.

"We recommended precast mosaic panels," Giardino said. "What (eventually came to look like) a design element was actually a change we recommended, a time-driven consideration to meet the new schedule."

BACK TO THE DRAWING BOARD

From the time Hillier representatives first put pen to paper, it took exactly five months to completely overhaul the design, complete the working drawings, achieve final approval from the State Education Department and inch closer to getting that critical first shovel in the ground.

"We started right around Christmas time and we were really churning," Chase said. "It was an incredible feat — are you kidding? An ($80) million project from zero? That project was a story for the whole world, with the time constraints, the budget, the design, the execution."

"We had very little time — between 90 and 120 days — to do the full working drawings," Chase said. "We were under the gun to get it done. But it was exciting. It was challenging for us."

Granto's prior "mobilization" efforts — namely, the HSQC and the "Power of One" group — would pay immediate dividends, setting the stage for a seamless transition to the new design team. Utilizing their critical input, Hillier's crew was literally able to "hit the ground running," Luaces said.

Consisting of students from both LaSalle and Niagara Falls, the team was organized beneath the umbrella of the national "Principles of Effectiveness," which prescribes strategies for "meeting the needs of the student as a customer."

The student representatives identified several main objectives: among them, ensuring a safe merger and identifying and resolving student issues and concerns. The group's input regarding environmental issues became as indispensable as the HSQC guidance on more physical aspects, Luaces said.

"In school work, that (camaraderie) is often very difficult to achieve," Luaces said, "but the community and the teachers were behind this (project). It had been organized extremely well, with the Quality Council helping to select materials, furniture, equipment. Carmen Granto essentially mobilized the entire district into a series of units" to help coordinate and plan a structure of maximum "usefulness" to all stake holders.

The building not only had to be "useful," but it needed to be "exciting," Chase said — "something very different from what was previously" planned.

"Our firm is known for design excellence, and we saw an opportunity with the vision of this board of education and school district to do something special, a vision for the future," Chase said.

"The school district pushed very hard for out-of-the-box thinking," Chase said. "Firms who design schools often get into a rut of designing boxes. They don't really get into vision and a mission for the future. The most difficult part (of this project) was designing a school that met the vision of the district for the future — and doing it within budget."

With the school board's blessing and the district's help, Hillier set out to design a building that defined the community, a building that issued a warm welcome, yet set the framework for the serious business taking place inside — the business of learning and growing and preparing for life beyond the walls of Niagara Falls High School.

It was a daunting task, but a task which Team Luaces nonetheless embraced with heart and soul. Luaces shared his philosophy with district officials.

"When it comes to high school facilities, society has been missing the boat in terms of the message we are sending to our children," Luaces said. "This project is going to reverse that trend."

Luaces took his inspiration from the teams working so diligently to see to it that this project lived up to its potential. He took his lead from Granto and the seven board members, whom he described as being "so out-there in terms of their thinking."

"They wanted a message sent: That a serious facility means business," Luaces said. "Yet the building should also impart a feeling of safety, of love."

For architect and project director Walter "Mac" Rawley, that meant creating "an open, safe environment with no hidden corners."

DESIGNING THE FUTURE

As a designer, Luaces embraces the fact that the eyes give us that all-important first impression. And this particular building would be scrutinized by many pairs of eyes, be they of the students, the staff, or the city itself.

Due to the unique circumstances of its conception, the project would also come under the microscope of the State Ed Department, the State Legislature, various labor unions, child advocacy groups and a curious educational community in general.

It was no overstatement to say that the world was watching on this one, and there could be no compromise. In addition to being functional, flexible and versatile in nature, the building also had to be striking and extraordinary in appearance. Absolutely nothing less would do.

For the designers, it all started with color.

Rawley said that designers initially sought an "earth tones" color scheme for the exterior of the building, something that would "blend with the land." The school would rise on the outskirts of sprawling Hyde Park, with its meandering creek and tranquil, tree-lined lake, a popular rest stop for scores of Mallard ducks and Canada geese. It would border the popular and scenic Hyde Park municipal golf course. For Luaces, it was important that the building fit in with those rustic surroundings.

Eventually opting for a "southwest" feel, designers settled on a fusion of sand and turquoise shades for the building's exterior, a cool combination that meshed well with the adjoining park lands.

Outer walls would be composed of mosaic panels in soothing sand, with contrasting trim around the windows. This was set off by tapering turquoise triangles and rounded roof contours, as well as pyramid-like skylights jutting majestically between the academic towers.

The building's interior would be significantly brighter and more vibrant, capitalizing on an abundance of natural light. Again, much of its "spirit" would emanate from the color scheme. Blue, red and yellow were chosen as the primary colors, choices that Rawley saw as significant.

The banked windows of an art classroom

"Some people think it's too elementary," he said. "I think it's great. The colors are very dynamic."

Eventually, it was decided to color-code the floors, with one color being dominant on each as a way to facilitate "way-finding" or location within the building. The first floor became predominantly red, the second floor blue, the third floor gold (yellow) and the fourth floor green.

That flooring, in fact, was one of the greatest benefactors from that Wicks legislation. With the $9 million saved, the district was able to significantly upgrade the flooring used for the building, moving from vinyl tiles to terrazzo, an improvement adding years of functional life to the building — and an additional $1 million to the bill.

Rawley steadfastly objects to complaints of the color scheme being "too elementary," but quickly admits that the philosophy behind it *was* elementary.

"High schools are typically difficult places to find your way around because they're usually large and irregular," Rawley said. "We wanted to create an understandable, sensible logic to the organization of the floors."

Hence, rooms of a particular type — business, science, and so on — were stacked one above another within each of the respective academic "houses."

"That way if someone is familiar with any floor — or familiar with the building at all — they could more easily find their way around," Rawley said.

In fact, each of the houses is structurally identical, architects having drawn up only one and then copying it three times via computer.

THE POWER OF REFLECTION

Given that the project was to be located in one of the energy capitals of the world, that theme — energy — became another of the building's central motifs.

"Energy is very much a part of this facility, in a philosophical way," Luaces explained. "(The building) reflects the energy associated with what goes into it: Dynamic, young individuals. The building celebrates that with its architecture. The architectural skin, the multi-level planes, the changes of material — we were trying to capture that energy of youth."

Not to mention the raw energy associated with the area's namesake waterfall, and the world-class hydroelectric generating facilities it spawned.

In fact, the new high school would essentially share segments of its landscape with the Robert Moses/Niagara Power Project. Granted, the coexistence was not openly evident, but a relationship had been established nonetheless.

"There are underground conduits (adjacent to the campus) running to the power plant," Luaces explained. "They're invisible to the eye, but the building reflects them and makes reference to them.

"The curved roofs, the end stairs that are wider at the top and taper toward the bottom. Hopefully, that all portrays to the person looking at it a sense of energy — like the falls themselves, and what happens in that area of the world. And the inside of the building, by the use of color and materials, captures that whole notion of energy. You can't look at that building and think anything but energy."

Of course, in the grand scheme of things, the building needed to reflect much more. It needed to represent a city on the rebound, a Rust Belt relic about to enjoy its renaissance.

An exterior view of the "new" Niagara Falls High School, showing the pre-cast mosaic panel walls

The onus for that was dropped squarely upon the shoulders of Luaces and company. He looked at it not as a burden, but a challenge.

"It is such a beautiful part of the world," he said of the scenic Niagara Falls setting. "But it is an area which has endured some (economic) hardship, and they need to bring industry back in order to attract development. If the building can help do that, I'll be very happy. I will have achieved my goal.

"I hope and pray to God that (the new school) will encourage development. It does put Niagara Falls in a different category. (Community developers) need to build off the fact that the city now has a Class A educational facility. Now they need to elevate the rest of the community to that standard. But I think this school will instill a feeling of hope in everybody. "

Such a fundamental change in the way residents looked at themselves and their community had to start somewhere, and planners realized the school presented the perfect opportunity.

"The private sector hasn't been able to initiate a lot of plans," said board member Don King. "So why not the school district?"

"It goes beyond just being a beautiful building," Luaces said. "A beautiful building is one thing, but if the people inside the beautiful building aren't happy, then we really haven't achieved much. They needed to feel when they walked in on that first day that they were ready to work, teach, and learn. And I believe we achieved that. It's a real comfortable place to work, to learn, to teach."

APART FROM THE REST

Luaces, a native of Cuba, began his architectural career a quarter-century ago designing colleges and universities. "I've been all over the place," he said, including some design work overseas.

Still, there were some distinctive features that set the Niagara Falls High School project apart from anything he'd done previously.

"First and foremost, the basic organization of the building into smaller components," he said. "We were creating a facility that was almost like having four distinct, small schools, each with its own administration. It was like the school was kind of broken down into a small city."

Despite its enormous size, and its imposing appearance from the outside, "the building is very compact, very efficient," Luaces said. "It celebrates the whole notion of smallness. The kids can identify with their own houses, be it by theme or by grade level.

"Each has its own lobby, its own distribution system (stairs), as opposed to just one grand lobby or public space."

The second unique feature: The prospect of technology playing a central role.

Granto envisioned each student being supplied a laptop computer, essentially linking that young adult with the world at large. And he foresaw the entire school being "wired" to accommodate that type of pursuit: the classrooms, the library, even the cafeterias.

All a student would need do would be to find a comfortable spot to sit and plug in, and the world would be at his or her fingertips. In fact, each classroom was outfitted with 31 data ports, as well as a television capable of receiving closed-circuit, cable and satellite feeds.

With technology providing such a central theme, "the media center became the focal point, then," Luaces said. It was placed in the center of the building — its heart — and would become the landmark feature.

"It was to be the hub, the big space in the center allowing everyone to familiarize themselves with where they were in the building," Luaces said. "As you walk into the building it becomes a space that is very transparent, where you can see from one side to the other. It creates a very large atrium, with technology in the center. That's why it is such a celebration of technology."

Providing students with the very best technology available was another means of elevating them to the planes of more affluent districts, King said.

"This school has absolutely the best, latest and fastest equipment money can buy," Rawley said. "Putting that technology into the hands of students is the best thing you can do … They will run with it. They'll do things we never conceived of. Every student has a computer that can be on any time they want, even at home."

With every student outfitted with a laptop computer, the kids will be able to come into the media center, plug into a port and tap into the Internet in order to research projects, access assignments or communicate with friends.

Luaces said the media center was designed with the flexibility to allow it to adapt to changing times. "It will change with time, as the times and technology changes," he said.

The building had to be designed in such a way as to permit maximum community access, while still preserving and protecting the instructional areas. Granto and the school board were dead-set firm on the fact that the building should be utilized as much as possible, by as many different segments of the community as possible.

For Luaces, that presented a bit of a dilemma: segregating areas that would be off-limits to the general public, using the facility after-hours.

Luaces accomplished this by designing "a very private side" — the classrooms — separated from "a very public side" — the theater and television studio, gymnasium and natatorium — by the central library area.

"There's nothing unique there, but it's clearly well organized," he said.

Those L-shaped towers can be locked off entirely, permitting use of the rest of the building while effectively sealing off the classroom area for security purposes.

THE NEO-PLASTICISM INFLUENCE

The interior of the building was inspired by one of Luaces' favorite artists: Piet Mondrian, a 19th century Dutch pioneer in the modernistic disciplines of Neo-Plasticism and Cubism. In his later years, Mondrian became renowned for his juxtaposition of colors and forms.

Mondrian's peculiar form of geometrical, abstract art came into prominence after World War II — and after the artist's death in 1944. Think of the patterns typically seen in such materials as ceramic floor tiles and linoleum, and you'll be thinking of Mondrian, whose designs have influenced everything from modern painting and sculpture to fashions.

Like a storybook scientist, Luaces set out to breathe life into Mondrian's images, to transport them from the flat page into the realm of the living and breathing.

"We transferred his work from the one-dimensional to the three dimensions of the building," Luaces said. "The inside of the building has a very different personality, a different feel (than the outside). It captures that whole notion of energy in a very different way.

"The floor areas in the corridor halls are an abstraction of Mondrian," Rawley said. "The whole interior scheme is based on an abstraction of his. We think it marries discipline and freedom. The discipline comes form the black and white, rectilinear patterns, the freedom from irregular splashes of colors."

A Hallway rotunda; notice the circular lighting above. Classroom wings "spoke" off from this common area

"The classrooms are atypical because they facilitate both independent and group work," Rawley said. "With this school we introduced the idea of the mini-lab, which is a common space between every pair of classrooms. This space allows teachers to work in 'team' configurations. After all, teams were the whole idea behind the thematic houses."

The mini-labs, or mini-conference rooms, allow students from classrooms on either side to gather in a common space and work together on joint ventures.

"Teachers can use it for remediation purposes while still maintaining the classroom setting," Luaces said. "We think of the classrooms as 'living rooms with a dining room.' It's approaching almost a small community setting. A family feel."

Designers consciously promoted and encouraged the idea of "family," the concept of sharing space and working together, Luaces said.

Even teachers can share in the "bonding," with rooms designed for teaming teachers to collectively prepare assignments and class plans.

The end result, according to administrative principal Philip Mohr, was "a school that bucks the trends in a lot of ways."

"Today you're always looking at high schools of 700 to 800 (population)," he said. "The contrary to that is out west — California, Arizona — but there weather is a big factor. They can have open campuses and so on," moves that alleviate some of the problems inherent with large student populations.

Niagara Falls High School planners achieved the "family" philosophy in a much different way.

"The whole idea here of taking a big building and making it feel small by creating houses and teams, with that we have de-departmentalized the high school," Mohr said. "There are no English or math or science wings. That was done for logistics and program reasons."

By keeping staffers in close proximity, "the staffers get to know each other better and they have time to collaborate, to develop personal relationships," Mohr said. "We wanted to train our teachers to be on the cutting edge, like Canada and England."

The "house" concept permitted students to "identify" with smaller social and academic groups within the building, planners said, which helped keep them from becoming lost in the shuffle.

Technology was the final piece of the puzzle, Mohr said.

"We've not only leveled the playing field" for students from all walks, Mohr said, "we've raised it to another level. Other districts are trying to catch up to us. Technology is truly one of the fundamental ways we are changing education.

"We're still growing into a lot if it," Mohr said. "But there has been some exemplary integration of technology into

Mike Kurilovitch

instruction. In all fairness, if we want to prepare kids for the world they'll be living in, we have to rely upon technology."

CHAPTER 7
REDESIGNING THE 3 R's

It wouldn't make much sense erecting a world-class facility to churn out students incapable of passing a physical examination, much less a college entrance exam. Carmen Granto knew it, everybody knew it. This was Niagara Falls' chance to do something special, and Granto seized the opportunity.

Calling on the Quality School Councils from each of the preexisting high schools, Granto issued them a very unique charge: help design the new school, but do so as if STUDENT LEARNING were the only objective. What conditions, what environment would be necessary to guarantee learning? What would such a school look like if cost were no object, if state mandates dictating such details as classroom size didn't exist?

"I told the board of education and the faculty that we would not spend eighty-some million dollars and still keep doing the same things," Granto recalled. "The definition of insanity is to keep doing things the same way and expect different results."

With that, the status quo was shown the door in Niagara Falls. The "educational delivery system" would be forever changed by a group that came to be known by four simple letters: HSQC.

On Feb. 11, 1997, Granto convened the first meeting of the group that would eventually become the "High School Quality Council." Utilizing concepts of the Total Quality Management process and applying the principles set forth in "Breaking Ranks," HSQC members set out to re-script the educational process.

"I gave them carte blanche," Granto said. "Study how high school kids learn. Ignore all state, federal and local policies and costs and just develop a program based on how kids learn. Then report back to me."

His instructions were intentionally vague. Yes, the building is important. But more so the environment. Tell us what it should be like. Granto stipulated that his role ended at bringing the two groups together; a budget had been established for their use and was totally within their control. They would answer to no one, but rather make recommendations to the superintendent, who would then pass them along to the school board.

The new group would set its own agenda, establish its own leadership, set its own calendar.

"The HSQC helped facilitate research," DiFrancesco said. "Rather than relying on opinions, they relied on good science. I believe they had a lot of good ideas. I only wish we had a little more money to implement all of them."

Tutored by nationally recognized educational consultant Dr. Lawrence Lezotte, the team was instructed to "examine ideas before making judgments."

"The new high school was not just new bricks and mortar," Lezotte reasoned. "It offered an opportunity for a new focus, new mission, new attitudes. Leadership was very important" and the HSQC accepted its role with open arms.

Their motto officially became "Learning for all, whatever it takes." Six simple words, one very complex mission.

Ultimately, the group forwarded to Granto some 175 recommendations, running the gamut from scheduling and teaching techniques to hiring practices, staff development and proper nutrition.

"Nearly every one of them (in actuality 133) was implemented by the board of education and myself," Granto said proudly.

The group wanted to see students do more hands-on work, something meaningful, something beneficial to the community as well as the student. Internships, apprenticeships and field studies were their suggestion — independent study monitored by community mentors — with credit granted for successful completion.

Check. In the very near future, in fact, required community service may become a condition for graduation.

The group recommended each student have an IEP (Individualized Education Plan) developed in conjunction with the student, his or her parents, counselors, teachers and possibly even a mentor, to assure that every student walking through those front doors received maximum educational benefit from the experience.

To do so meant having a safe environment: as such, HSQC suggested a ban on student backpacks and the use of personal locks on lockers. They also recommended the school employ a number of "security personnel," each of whom would be "dressed for immediate identification."

Check and check.

Among many other topics, the HSQC also looked at physical-education requirements, "seat time" and other "crazy kinds of stuff" dictated by state and federal mandates.

"The biggest obstacle (to fundamental reform) were the state regulations," Granto said. "All these regulations make (schools) like a factory. The bricks-and-mortar stuff, in relation to that, was easy. Changing attitudes — that's going to take some time."

One of the HSQC's main goals — as well as the district's — was to eliminate the "series of locked steps" leading to graduation at a prescribed age, as opposed to graduation once sufficient experience had been gained to move on.

"We didn't want compulsory attendance but compulsory learning," Granto said. "Attendance drives (state) aid, which drives money. We're switching now, hopefully, to learning. The state is moving toward that but it's taking time."

After all, if increased student learning were not the goal, then the spectacular new high school would be just another pretty building, contributing little more to the community than sprucing up an unsightly, overgrown field.

In early December, 1998, the first-ever NFHS-LSHS joint faculty meeting was held. Some 200 people attended.

The 32-member High School Quality Council (HSQC) had already been meeting officially for some two months. The team of teachers, administrators, students, parents and community representatives had been exploring particulars in the areas of context, content, teaching and learning.

They dissected the "theme towers" planned for the new school, Lezotte said. They wanted to assure a balance within each tower — racial, ethnic, gender — and they sought to guarantee cross-tower interaction. Otherwise, the math/science/technology tower might end up an "elitist" wing, attracting only the most academically gifted students, while the visual and performing arts tower might end up on the other end of the spectrum, being viewed as an "easy out" for lesser achievers.

It was even suggested that, given the nature of the Niagara Falls community, the district should consider a "tourism" theme for one of the towers. Students would receive instruction focusing on the intricacies of the hospitality industry, in preparation for the procurement of jobs in that trade upon graduation.

They went so far as to suggest that such a program could foster partnerships with segments of the local hotel, airline and hospitality industries, allowing for internships and practical, hands-on experience.

WHO LET THE WOLVERINES OUT?

Team member Rich Meranto, a teacher at NFHS, explained that team members also looked at "what we (had), what we should have and what we need" in terms of sports and student activities.

The "coming together" of the two populations was a major point of focus, as were such issues as school culture and climate, and the name, motto and colors for the new building.

As Granto had predicted so many months before, naming the school turned into a 12-round affair with the three-knockdown rule waived.

"The name was a big issue," DiFrancesco said. Elements from the two former schools wanted their identities preserved in some manner. Instead of the Niagara Falls Power Cats, for instance, they preferred the LaSalle Power Cats ... or maybe the Niagara Falls Explorers.

Ultimately, it was decided to maintain the "Niagara Falls" designation, while seeking a clean slate with the school mascot and colors.

"LaSalle felt sold out," DiFrancesco said, "but the simple fact is, there is no place called LaSalle, USA."

Student input was pivotal in deciding upon the mascot — the Wolverines — and the team colors, which matched the yellow and blue of the University of Michigan. The school logo (a wolverine leaping through the letters "NF") was designed by art teacher Len Rusin (LSHS).

Team name: scrappy. Team colors: snappy. A sure recipe for athletic success, if ever there was one.

Back in the HSQC camp, the "teams" went their own separate ways to explore their particular assignments. One team examined the ways in which people learn, including research on the brain. Another team examined the best practices and methods for teaching. Input was solicited from other districts which had combined two school populations within a single building.

Within a couple of months, the HSQC had recommended implementation of four academic "themes" within the school's four towers, although the themes were not immediately determined. Possibilities considered at the time included traditional topics like math and science, as well as more non-traditional fare as "citizenry" and "the future."

Public forums — remember those? — were slated over a three-week period, allowing the public input on educational issues pertaining to the new school.

Citing obsolescence of textbooks as a growing problem, Granto floated the idea of outfitting each of the new school's 2,500 students with a laptop computer. What was originally seen as pie-in-the-sky ultimately became reality, with the district issuing "free" IBM Think Pad laptops to every students walking through the doors, courtesy of the "IBM ThinkPad At School" lease program.

The school district currently provides free Internet access to all staff, students, and their families. In September 2003, thanks to a 10-year agreement with the local cable company, parents with access to cable television will be able to view their children's grades via their TV at any time.

"All the technology brought change along with it," DiFrancesco said. "It's a research tool, the kind of thing needed (to help kids) move on to the world of work and higher education.

"It opened up a world to our kids, much more so than many would ever have seen otherwise. Some of it was good and some was bad. The lesson we learned was that the Internet puts the world at the fingertips of our youngsters."

With the world at a kid's fingers, it was thought that it might be a good idea to have an adult at their shoulder, looking over to assure their computer usage was appropriate. In the end, DiFrancesco said, an "acceptable use policy" was developed and students were given the responsibility of "self-policing."

In late 1998, the district distributed surveys to students in grades 7-12, as well as faculty members and residents, seeking additional input on the high school. The goal was to collect opinions on what elements were necessary for a "21st Century School."

While all this study was taking place, steps were also being taken to gradually merge ongoing student activities at the two high schools. The first groups to consolidate were the drama clubs and marching bands, which combined forces at the outset of 1999. Sports teams, understandably, were more gradually blended.

The HSQC focused upon the first 30 days of life inside the new school, seeing it as an opportunity to "set the culture" and assure that a golden opportunity to affect change wasn't lost in the shuffle, Lezotte said.

Meranto told the Niagara Gazette that the opening of the new school represented "the ending of two cultures and the bringing together of a new culture, and all the rites of passage have to take place."

Take place they did — and in no small manner, thanks in large part to the members of the HSQC.

Through it all, team members were well aware of the spotlight beaming upon them throughout their deliberations.

"Everybody's watching us — the state, the community, other school districts," team member Ida Massaro (teacher, LSHS) said. "That's scary. The whole thing is an experiment."

But it was a glorious, wonderful, crazy experiment that resulted in many fundamental changes to the way business was traditionally conducted.

Getting It Done

Take the concept of teaming, for instance. Long thought to be exclusively "middle-school" in nature, teaming has worked at the high school, in no small measure due to the fact that teachers embraced the idea.

Those small "work areas" between classrooms helped facilitate the concept; teacher accommodations also played a role, making collaboration easier and more tenable.

A classroom showing at rear the "common" area shared between rooms, used for conferencing, remediation and small-group learning

WHAT ABOUT AN OXYGEN CHAMBER?

Teaming was one of the HSQC's more practical recommendations. Others were more, well, more unusual.

Citing studies touting the benefits of such a move, the group sought to have pure oxygen pumped into the building. That prospect turned out to be slightly beyond the means of the district.

Likewise, the HSQC wanted plenty of fresh water available for students and staffers. While it isn't bottled fresh at the source, that one was accomplished. And not only water is available, but also a selection of sodas and fruit juices.

Said executive chief administrator Philip Mohr: "Visitors are very often surprised by the number of pop machines in the building. But that comes down to pouring rights. The (soda) machines go on at 3 p.m., but juice and water is available all day. Students are permitted to carry water to classes."

Another HSQC initiative: theme specialists. Teachers dedicated to the premise of promoting the "themes" of each academic house, acting as liaisons between teachers and administration.

"When you talk about changing culture, theme specialists are a new anomaly," Mohr said, "and there are a lot of misconceptions.

"They are service providers to teachers. They help connect what teachers are doing to the themes of the particular houses. They work with the teachers during planning/collaboration time and also oversee staff development, mentoring and technology."

Said Mohr: "We literally started on the ground floor with theme specialists. They set a high-energy direction for the building. They are not mandated, but I truly believe them to be the cornerstone of the instructional program. We need to protect theming.

"We've done a lot of atypical high school things ... and the theme specialists had a great impact in changing perspectives in that regard."

"To most kids (the theme specialists) were and probably still are invisible," DiFrancesco said. "They are *not* direct providers to students. They support teachers in the classrooms and *then* kids benefit in that way."

The deans of students had the most visibility, the most direct impact on kids, DiFrancesco said, "especially in terms of discipline." The principals worked with the community, with school support staff and teachers, evaluating the classrooms and managing the building.

"It would have been much easier if we'd just closed the two schools and moved the students and equipment into the new school," Mohr told reporters. "But we're also making cultural changes and it is very evident in the academic team. We're working differently than any of us have ever worked before."

The idea of four principals helps promote a feeling of "smaller, individual" schools within a larger building, he said.

"The whole school is based on teams," Mohr said, "and we are a team of administrators. All with very different, but equally valuable styles, based on our backgrounds."

Flex scheduling was another area studied, with the intention of accommodating those who prefer to either sleep late or start the day earlier and thus finish early.

According to HSQC research, studies have shown that high school kids perform better later in the day, meaning that a later start would be advantageous for some. While flexible scheduling has been employed to a degree, logistics have limited its wide-scale implementation.

"It's unfortunate that lunch and transportation very often drive the schedule at any school," Mohr said. "For four out of our eight periods we are serving lunch." Manipulating schedules would offer "a great advantage to this building," he said, but it would also require longer contractual work days, fewer lunch periods and more staffing — conditions unlikely to be met within the current economic climes.

"It is not a dead issue, though," Mohr said. "We will continue to explore it. We may try to start within one house."

"One of the best, most contemporary ideas was the laptops," school board member Don King said. "Not just as an instructional instrument ... but for helping to teach kids respect and responsibility. That's as important a lesson as the three R's. Add rights, respect and responsibility and you have the six R's.

"That was really a visionary concept for the kids. And the real worth of it is just starting to take hold in the community ... many of these kids would never have an opportunity to take something like that home on a daily basis."

To ease the transition for students, a "help desk" was established in the library for students having difficulties with their new laptops.

Granto said that the advantages technology offered students — and teachers, and even the family cat, for that matter — went well beyond convenience.

Take biology, for instance. "They can do virtual dissections with a computer," Granto said. "You don't have to bring the cat in anymore."

As part of its deliberations, the HSQC even made liberal use of the mock classroom which had been erected at LaSalle, designed to give visitors the "feel" of what rooms in the new school would be like.

Such was life in the HSQC: affecting change, whatever it took.

"The HSQC process was grueling," Mohr said. "There were a lot of agendas and personal interests coming to the table ... even (with) good-hearted, professional, well-intending people. Change is hard."

He credited people like Dr. Lezotte with providing the "monumental leadership" necessary to see the process through.

"We had to build a treasure chest of beliefs, and we're talking about lofty goals, so it isn't always a pleasant, fun experience. It didn't happen easily."

After all, there were 30-35 people at HSQC meetings, each with the intention of "stirring the mud up at the bottom of the pond (so we could) reevaluate it. Everything was up for discussion. We were routing the comfortable from their roosts."

Now that the mud is resettling, it's becoming apparent that perhaps more, still, needs to be done, Mohr said.

"Most advocates of change say you can't tinker with a system, you have to blow it up and redevelop," Mohr said. "Maybe we still need to do more."

HSQC member Eisha Basit may have summed up the feelings of all her cohorts, boiling down her sentiments to a mere two sentences.

"I watched people argue and pull their hair, drink lots and lots of coffee and then make up with each other. Being involved with creating a school has been an experience I will never forget, but going to it will be an even greater experience."

CHAPTER 8
BREAKING GROUND ON A GROUNDBREAKING VENTURE

July 20, 1998. The day broke clear and warm and by mid-morning only thin, streaky puffs interrupted the infinite blue above.

Ground breaking day. And never did that moniker seem more appropriate than for this particular occasion.

As the festivities commenced, Granto trotted out one of his favorite expressions: "Onward and upward."

"Without a doubt, the spirit of this will forever leave an indelible mark on this community," he said. "It shows that when people work together, good things can happen. With this school, we're onward and upward."

A noontime crowd of 350 cheered on a handful of students from both high schools as their chrome-plated shovels, flashing in the brilliant sunshine, collectively turned the earth — and in the process turned a page in Niagara Falls history.

Behind them, the combined high school band played for the first time, decked out in fanciful new uniforms paid for using $55,000 from an exclusive "pouring rights" deal with a prominent soft drink company. Afterward, a cheer went up that seemed to meld relief with sheer joy that the project was finally taking shape, and would soon be ready to welcome its first class.

Mayor James Galie, surveying the site, proudly agreed that it was a "terrific" spot for a school, bounded by the rolling green waves of the golf course and trees of every description.

"I thank and applaud the City Council for approving the lease to make this happen," he said.

Less than three weeks remained until the special legislation's sunset clause took effect, but no one was thinking about that now. It was finally shovel-in-the-ground time.

Once the crowds had left the construction crews took over. As many as 400 worked simultaneously on the site at peak moments. Good weather conditions contributed to a quick start on construction and by Oct. 1, the gaping basement had been dug. Shortly thereafter the skeleton of the building began to take shape.

Gradually, the "L" shapes of the academic wings became noticeable and the auditorium went from resembling an open-air coliseum to an impressive, fan-shaped hulk. The building was finally coming to life!

"One of the biggest challenges was the construction schedule itself," said Ciminelli's Giardino. "It was 18 months from ground-breaking to ribbon-cutting for an almost 400,000 square foot building featuring glass curtain walls and some very unique amenities within."

A view during construction of the Performing Arts Center in the "new" Niagara Falls High School

Granto said that Ciminelli did a commendable job balancing the many duties inherent with managing the project.

"These guys were charged with keeping the project on schedule and on budget, with ordering materials and coordinating a lot of different sub-contractors," Granto said. "Originally the pool was in, then it was out, then back in.

"By that time we had already built the end wall, so that was a little bit of a problem. (Putting the pool back into the design) added $2.4 million to the cost."

That probably qualified as one of the "lose some" moments to which Rollins had alluded earlier.

"The district determined it had needs after we had already begun construction," Giardino said. "We had to find ways to accommodate them."

The Olympic-sized swimming pool inside the school natatorium

Accommodating an Olympic-sized pool, for instance, meant not only designing a pool to fit the available space, but one that was affordable. Then there was the matter of rescheduling construction.

It wasn't exactly the most preferable way to go about building one of the world's greatest school buildings.

"We built the bridge as we crossed the river," Granto said, a classic understatement.

Other items built "on the run" included the clock tower added to the face of the Performing Arts Center ($15,000 plus another $3,000 for clock installation; and two aluminum plaques inside the main entrance, one recognizing the workers on the project, another the HSQC members — a hit of $6,000.

An extra $1 million was spent to outfit the school hallways with epoxy-coated concrete block walls for extra durability. The material is considered the strongest surface short of stainless steel.

The project's exemption from sales tax on all materials was critical in that respect, saving tons of money and enabling the use of top quality materials throughout, such as terrazzo instead of vinyl for floors, not to mention those glazed hall tiles.

There were other minor glitches but they failed to throw the project off course. A small section of diesel-fuel contaminated soil, found during excavation for water and sewer lines, was quickly removed. The area was then cleared by state Department of Environmental Conservation and the state Health Department. Cost of the setback: $50,000 to remediate the site.

PROBLEM — WHAT PROBLEM?

The major glitch — the switch in architects — hadn't just meant a new set of drawings from which to work, Rollins said. The change in attitude was even more remarkable.

"It was immediate and very visible," he said. "And it wasn't just one person. (Hillier) showed up at meetings with four people — the heads of all their divisions. And they showed up with plans and time lines: 'This is how we get from here to here'."

"They really started from scratch, just reprogramming the whole building. The tact they used with people — a very no-nonsense, down-to-earth approach, very negotiable — it kind of disarmed people. It was fabulous. They showed up with a process, the right people and a plan, and it made all the difference in the world."

Getting It Done

"I'm probably their biggest champion, but I'm also probably their biggest critic, as well. I was always challenging them to be better: with deliverables, time frames, the product and the quality of the product. They were hired on my recommendation, so that gave me a vested interest in them succeeding. Still, I've been very critical when they haven't (met expectations)."

The "fast-track" nature of the project resulted in some glitches, most notably a breakdown in communications, Rollins said. Consequently, the type of refrigerant used in the building's chillers wasn't the type planners had wanted. Originally, only eight "data drops" were installed in each classroom, although the district had requested 32.

"That was a misunderstanding that kind of fell between the cracks," Rollins said, and one which was rectified at significant expense.

"We had many of those (change-orders) in the construction process," Rollins said, "probably mostly due to the time frame. Normally, to design a building like this — the size and cost and the technical nature of the building — you would expect to sign an architect for at least one year, maybe 18 months, for the design process. In five-and-a-half months (problems like that) were inevitable, but nothing insurmountable, nothing of a critical nature.

"In fact, we were able to value-engineer the building along the way. We found ways to save money. We probably cut out $2 million along the way."

Actual construction proceeded virtually without incident. There was only one major injury, coming in the early stages when a worker tripped and was impaled on a concrete reinforcement bar. He survived, but lawsuits are expected.

Even change orders — a problem that usually adds about 10 percent to the original contract price on a project of this size, Rollins said — were not an issue. Figures showed that changes came in slightly under six percent for the NFHS project, a fact Rollins attributed to "picking the right contractor."

"They were extremely fair," he said. "They truly were team players. If this had been a public bid situation you would have had a stack of change orders that high — you couldn't have gotten through them in a year. But this was a team environment. We were all on the same team and we all had the same goal — delivering a beautiful facility for the City of Niagara Falls."

It happened because Rollins, like all those before him, did his homework.

"Oh yeah, up front," he said. "I wasn't about to fail. This was a brand-new venture for Honeywell, and I wasn't about to crash and burn. I went out and got the best team possible. I stacked the deck a little bit, no question there. But history will show this was a great project."

Rollins attributed that to the "no B.S. leadership of Carmen Granto."

"There really hasn't been a down side at all," he said. "It's been so refreshing and rewarding, personally. But there were a couple of anxious moments ..."

Such as the time when the sunset clause was creeping up and the project was "out of time, over budget and at the twelfth hour," Rollins said.

"We needed to break ground before the sunset clause on the legislation expired," he recalled, "and (Gary) Bichler (of Ciminelli) and I were just pulling our hair out trying to find places to cut to bring it into budget.

"We didn't have any time to send Hillier back to the drawing board, so Carmen Granto made the tough decision to pull the pool out at the time. That was a $2 million savings right there. Then we reduced the landscaping significantly, and there were more decisions on some mechanical issues."

When the city "reneged on its promise to renovate the pool at Sal Maglie (Stadium), Carmen put money from the Power Authority back into the pool at the school," Rollins said. The Power Authority later objected to "putting money into the school," Rollins said, and officials subsequently identified "contingency funds" to cover the costs of the pool addition.

"That's another story to be told," Rollins said of the contingency budget. Bristling over newspaper accounts that costs had spiraled, Rollins said that the report, citing a source "very high up in the State Ed department," was "horribly untrue and unfair."

Getting It Done

"To bring a project like this in under 10 percent contingency is next to miraculous," he said. "We've just been very lucky."

He attributed the State Ed dissatisfaction to being "cut out of the loop in this type of project."

"The two gyms, the terrazzo floors, the six-lane pool, the 1,700-seat theater, those were bells and whistles that drove the per-square-foot cost up," Rollins said. "But that's no one's business. It didn't cost State Ed anything. We didn't ask the state for any more money."

GIVING CREDIT WHERE CREDIT'S DUE

Rollins said that numerous individuals and companies deserve accolades for bringing the Niagara Falls High School project to fruition.

"Honeywell will be recognized for successful management of the project, the Hillier Group will undoubtedly receive a design award for the building, and the contractor stands to be recognized by one or several different organizations," he said "They will receive significant recognition. And the Niagara Falls School District deserves kudos for an unbelievable facility at no increase in public taxes, and for delivering the project on-time and on-budget."

Even the politicians deserve applause, Rollins said, not to mention local labor leaders who "took some heat from around the state for supporting the legislation, which wasn't a very popular thing for them to do."

As for his own involvement, he downplayed the role with a car maker analogy:

"We make the car," he said, "and then hand the keys over to the customer."

In Don King's opinion, Hillier deserves the lion's share of the praise. Changing architects mid-stream was easily the biggest obstacle encountered in the entire project, he said, yet the transition was handled professionally and without major disruption.

Next to that, King said, the changing of school district attorneys was the next biggest headache.

Massaro and James Roscetti were brought in at a critical point in the proceedings after the district's previous lawyers left for reasons unrelated to the school project.

Massaro and Roscetti, too, had to hit the ground running, clearing up such "inconsequential" issues as alienation of park lands and the ownership of the new school, among others.

Another snag, another pothole on the road to achievement. But in the end, nothing more than another detour successfully negotiated.

CUTTING THE RIBBON

By the time August, 2000 had rolled around, the buzz around the city was inescapable. Construction was virtually complete and the grand opening was just around the corner.

The din reached a crescendo on Thursday, August 30 when the media was introduced to the school during an exclusive noontime walk-through. Realizing that some skepticism lingered in pockets of the community, school district representatives had brain stormed a gala grand-opening for the new building, a four-day-long celebration appropriately — and conveniently — coinciding with Labor Day weekend.

School board president Don King, Niagara Falls Area Chamber of Commerce president Charles Steiner and retired school district administrator Marilyn Lojek were assigned key roles in coordinating the activities.

The public portion of the event got underway Friday morning with an invitation-only "educational breakfast" in the school's main gymnasium.

Assemblyman Pillittere, a key player in achieving the legislation which made the project possible, stepped to the podium and elicited laughs from the crowd with a tale from the political arena.

"About eight years ago I got a visit from (former school district attorney) Mike Gold and (chief school business officer) Roy Rogers about this crazy idea they had to build a school with a public-private partnership," he began. "I think the only reason state staff met with us was because they wanted to see if there really was a guy named Roy Rogers."

NFHS co-ed Christina Andrejcak conveyed things from the student standpoint.

"Finally," she said, "a school where I can play varsity soccer without riding my bike 20 blocks to get to the field. Finally, a school where I can look up at the ceiling and not worry about the liquid dripping down on my head. This new building will give everybody a chance to learn and grow together."

Parent and school volunteer Aleeta Zornek put the matter into a wider perspective.

"The new high school will offer a reason for people to move into the city, not escape it," she said. "To all of you who said it would never happen, my message is 'Believe it'."

The ribbon was officially cut at high noon, followed immediately afterward by student-guided tours of the new facility. The event came complete with shuttle bus service from several points to alleviate traffic congestion. Tours ran every 15 minutes, and the response was so overwhelming that Granto hastily arranged to extend the program into the upcoming week.

Complementing the tour was a video presentation staged in the auxiliary gymnasium, addressing many "frequently-asked questions" about the project and hopefully filling any gaps remaining after the tours.

Capping the day's events were an afternoon reception featuring the croonings of NFHS alumnus Michael Civisca and a 7 p.m. concert by the Academic Festival Orchestra, which included members of the Buffalo Philharmonic Orchestra and acclaimed opera singer Maria Fortuna, another Niagara Falls native.

On Saturday, Sept. 2 the new stadium was dedicated and the football Wolverines debuted, dropping a decision to state powerhouse (and eventual state champion) Jamestown. Although the team couldn't provide many during the contest, the district staged an impressive display of fireworks afterwards, pleasing those remaining from the standing-room-only crowd.

Surveying the weekend's events, board member Don King couldn't help but smile.

"The celebration should go on forever and forever, as far as I'm concerned," he said. "It's been a long time coming."

There was no shortage of praise during the educational breakfast as a succession of speakers applauded the district and all others involved in bringing the school to life.

Speaking before 1,000 people in the Performing Arts Center, Representative John LaFalce lauded the district for closing the "digital divide" between the haves and have-nots.

"Technology more than any other factor has powered the economic growth of the past half-dozen years or so," he said. "But there's a problem — the digital divide. Those who 'have' are accessing technology and using it, and those who 'don't have' are not. Here in Niagara Falls, (people) said 'we will not only ... close the divide, we will obliterate the divide.'"

Louis Ciminelli, patriarch of the general contracting firm, spoke glowingly of the project and his delight to be "walking down the road as pioneers"

U.S. Undersecretary for Education Judith Winston also addressed the gathering.

"This is the place where the next Bill Gates could easily emerge," she said. "If I was interested in going back to high school, I would like to be right here, at Niagara Falls High School."

That said, she cautioned those who would be using the building to be sure to get the most from it.

"Education is more than just the setting in which it occurs, so you are to be commended for putting as much thought into what goes into the building," she said. "It's not just an architectural marvel, not just an example of state-of-the-art technology, not just a facility for the community. See this as a means to an end, a vessel for a higher quality education."

Sunday morning featured an inter-denominational service highlighted by motivational vignettes from various school district alumni. The weekend culminated with a "Salute To Labor" picnic on Monday afternoon, open to all labor union members who participated in construction of the project, as well as all district personnel.

Larry Lezotte, who played such a prominent role in the development of the school, summed up the feelings of many of those in attendance.

"As an educational reformer, I'd like to suggest the opening of the high school could not have come at a better time. The call for educational reform has made its way to the top of the political agenda. This high school will be a lighthouse for high schools throughout New York and the nation."

CHAPTER 9

NIAGARA FALLS HIGH SCHOOL: A VIRTUAL TOUR

For the benefit of those who couldn't make it first-hand for the grand opening festivities, a virtual walk-through is the next best thing ... within the confines of the printed page, anyway. Just look at it this way: at least you're guaranteed the best guides.

And who better to lead our "tour" than the proud father himself, "Mac" Rawley?

Rawley can't help but beam as he gestures toward his "baby," the new Niagara Falls High School. In youthful vernacular, it was a "crib" that consumed some 18,000 cubic yards of concrete for the foundation alone; another 1,670,000 pounds of reinforcing steel to hold it all together. It rose to life boasting 6,500 light fixtures, some 900 doors and a whopping 7,717 panes of glass (or 72,298 square feet).

Ten miles worth of metal framing was needed for its voluminous windows. Nearly 200 miles of wiring was installed to handle the building's power demands, and another 285 miles worth to handle security, sound, the fire alarm system and the many computers. By the way, there's also two miles of multi-strand fiber optics.

Those fancy floors? Try 340,000 masonry blocks set in a staggering 1.1 million pounds of grout and 2.6 million pounds of mortar.

Overseeing it all, with an eye toward student safety: 62 video cameras and some 200 motion detectors.

Think you would've gotten that kind of detailed information from a fresh-faced freshman?

Rawley quotes it all in great detail as he explains the thought processes which went into the decisions, the objectives architects had in mind for particular design elements. Triumphantly he chronicles the design changes which saved money and conserved space.

Getting It Done

At one time a hardhat was necessary for this exclusive tour; now all one need do is thumb through the following pages ...

Adjacent to the main entrance is the entrance to the school's Performing Arts Center

THE AUDITORIUM

If the new high school were to indeed become a community center, a rallying point, a showcase, then the auditorium would be a key component. After all, what message is sent by an auditorium that doubles as a gymnasium?

From the very beginning, organizers and designers knew that the auditorium had to be special, and the final product reflects that in its grandeur.

Mike Kurilovitch

A view from the rear of the stunning Performing Arts Center of the "new" Niagara Falls High School

"The idea was that it should be capable of taking in commercial road shows, as well as school productions," Rawley says. "Music, dance, drama. It had to be flexible and functional."

The auditorium — "we prefer to call it the "Performing Arts Center'," Rawley says — was designed with a seating capacity of 1,750, each comfortably upholstered seat offering not only arm rests, but a delightfully unobstructed view of the mammoth stage.

The theater was designed with a separate loading dock, just off the main stage, and a motorized lift adjacent to the stage. "It offers the same kind of accommodations as a Shea's (a premier commercial theater in Buffalo) only not as large," says Rawley.

Features include an orchestra pit, a full-function stage and fly tower and 25 line sets; commodious control room; two spacious dressing rooms, with 12 seats in each of the toilet facilities; and outside broadcasting and recording capabilities.

Getting It Done

Large wall and ceiling panels lend an impressive acoustic presence, in spite of the room's imposing size.

Theatergoers enjoy ample parking facilities adjacent to the theater, a two-story lobby designed to handle substantial box office and concession stand traffic, and convenient elevator access in the main lobby.

In fact, the entire facility is handicapped accessible, including the 50-seat orchestra pit.

"It was intended to function as a stand-alone center," Rawley says of the theater. Six entrances allow for maximum circulation and safety, yet access to the remainder of the school is easily restricted, so the theater can be operated independently.

After all, he says, "it is unusual for high schools to be able to take in or produce commercial shows."

Another view of the Performing Arts Center, this time with the sunken orchestra pit (left)

Mike Kurilovitch

Alongside the main theater is a "black box theater" which doubles as a self-contained television studio — not to mention a convenient rehearsal space when pinched for room.

Nearby chorus and band rooms — conveniently segregated from the classroom wings to effectively reduce noise problems — offer additional dressing or rehearsal options in the event of extremely large productions.

"The main idea with the (black box) facility was that we would be able to broadcast events like conferences and special appearances to schools throughout the district via the district-wide video network," Rawley notes.

"It's really for video broadcasting and recording. It's fully equipped with theatrical lighting, sound and recording equipment."

Performing Arts Center lobby, which includes ticket window and snack bar

Getting It Done

THE LIBRARY/MEDIA CENTER

A two and-a-half story, glass-enclosed capsule boasting natural light compliments of two large skylights, the centralized library/information/technology center is referred to as "The Media Center" in recognition of its many critical roles.

It is the hub from which the classroom wing "spokes" are generated, and is designed to resemble a futuristic space craft — the school's private connection to the future.

Rawley notes that the building's outer walls would not have permitted sufficient light to filter into the center core, so arcing triangular skylights were employed in the ceiling, looking like miniature pyramids rising into the clouds.

The light is then "filtered" through glass to lend a warm, welcoming feel.

The media center houses the hardware for the district's video system, as well as its data network. It provides both LAN (local area) and WAN (wide area) networks and from it, the district can transmit educational programming throughout the school, the district, even the world.

In a more traditional sense, the library's first floor boasts some 20,000 books, radially arranged in a circular fashion, along with 50 computer work stations. It is fully capable of hosting two classes at once, with each student hooked up to the Internet via connections at the work station tables.

The outer "shell" of the school's circular Media Center, viewed from a second floor walkway

Mike Kurilovitch

The second floor functions as a reading room, offering informal seating at individual study tables. It is also formulated "in the round" and takes full advantage of the aforementioned natural sunlight.

CLASSROOM WINGS

The four academic "towers" offer unique areas of academic concentration: Liberal Arts and Drama, Science and Technology, Business and Enterprise, Sports and Hospitality. Each has its own lobby at the entrances.

"That allows us to break the school down into four groups of about 600 kids each," Rawley explains, "so you have a smaller community and a greater sense of community. Each house contains all four grades."

A view down one of the classroom "wings"

Getting It Done

The towers are composed of classroom "suites" — two classrooms of 1,000 square feet apiece, each with a capacity of 25 students — connected in the middle by glass-enclosed "conference rooms" or mini-labs.

The state-of-the-art teleconference room/amphitheatre, which features Internet access and microphone at each seat and scanning video cameras

With a capacity of eight to 10 persons, the labs are designed to facilitate teacher conferences, breakout groups, small-group learning and special project work.

Classroom desks are outfitted with individual data and power outlets for each student, wired through the desks for convenience and safety but with full reconfiguration possibilities.

Business classrooms are slightly larger at 1,200 square feet in order to accommodate business machines and larger desks. Fundamentally, they operate the same as regular classrooms, although each offers desktop computers to facilitate the Computer Aided Drafting (CAD) program.

Retractable video screens retreat into recessed housing in the ceilings of the business rooms.

The Special-Education Center features a pair of "self-contained" classrooms, each with a kitchen, toilet and shower, and with a mock bedroom workshop for basic skills training.

The Counseling Center boasts six offices for the counselors and psychologist, as well as a reception area.

There are five art rooms — 1,200 square feet apiece — located on the west side of the library, with two-story sculpture spaces on the first floor and photography and computer graphics labs on the second floor, overlooking the adjacent golf course.

The third floor features a pair of futuristic-looking, "long-distance learning" centers with capacities of 125 people that can easily and effectively double as video-teleconference centers, with full closed-circuit transmission and reception capabilities.

Identified by their sweeping, curved steps that house rows of circular tables with swing-out seats, the distance learning lab boasts cameras that automatically (via strategically placed microphones) focus in on any audience member asking a question or speaking — a special feature enabling "personal interaction" with a teacher who may be a whole world away.

These side-by-side amphitheaters can be combined into one large space. Data and power outlets are available at each seat. Images from individual laptops can be projected onto the screen to facilitate "personalized" instruction.

"It's comparable to some professional corporate conference centers that I've done," Rawley says. "Far above any other school I've ever been involved with."

Even the fire stairs were given deep thought.

"Light and access were two major concerns," Rawley says. "We wanted hiding spaces and blind corners minimized" for safety purposes. In the final product, "the stairs are not dead spaces," he says. "They will be used all the time, as the primary path of vertical circulation for students."

GYMNASIUM

Another "flexible" facility, designed for student use during the daytime and for community use at night, whether as an athletic facility or an auditorium.

The exhibition gymnasium seats 2,200, split between a permanent upper section and two retractable lower tiers of bleachers.

Quiet for now, but the "Wolvarena" erupts with over 2,000 screaming fans for home games of the school's powerful basketball team.

An enclosed track circles the entire top of the gym, occasionally looking in through window spaces. It features a rubberized athletic surface.

The six-lane, Olympic-size pool features a movable bulk head capable of adjusting the length of racing lanes between 25 meters and 75 feet. It is also equipped for diving, permitting district students to compete in that event for the first time ever. Seating is available for 300 spectators.

A separate entrance/lobby area allows the gymnasium areas to be used independently from the classroom wings. The lobby features a separate box office and concession stand for use during sporting events.

Both the exhibition gymnasium and the auxiliary "practice" gym feature rubber athletic floor coverings mounted over maple hardwood, the surfaces designed to minimize impact on the knees and joints during physical exertion.

"It gives a bit of a cushion, a springiness," Rawley notes. "It's much better for the ankles and joints" than hardwood flooring, not to mention "much safer," he said.

Other facilities: a wrestling room, weight training room and fitness center and spacious lockers and coaches offices.

CAFETERIA

In this building, even the dining rooms must be multi-functional. As such, not only are they equipped with the typical long tables and bench seating, but they, too, offer data port outlets so students can "plug in" while filling up.

"It's a cyber-cafe, in effect," Rawley says. "The four dining rooms also double as testing centers and study halls.

"We increased our available funding for this school substantially by getting the dining rooms designated as study rooms," Rawley notes. "They have to meet certain criteria in order for that to happen."

The dining rooms can also be used to accommodate community organizations for their events. They're all fully equipped with drinking fountains, food service and toilet facilities to accommodate 150 people.

One can even be sealed off for use as a dinner theater. Operated cooperatively, the dining rooms can be combined to accommodate banquets for up to 2,400 people.

Sharing a single service area just off the central kitchen, the dining rooms are arranged "like a corner deli," Rawley comments, employing kiosks to offer a lo carte items such as ice cream, potato chips and candy in addition to the traditional luncheon fare.

"That's so people needing just a little something don't have to go through the full lunch lines," Rawley says.

The kitchen was designed as its own entity, with a separate loading dock offering abundant room for box trucks to pull in and make instant deliveries.

"That way they can unload in comfort during the winter months," Rawley says.

Janitors are taken into consideration with about 15 large closets — one for every 30,000 square feet of building space. There's even room for a police substation just off the dining room area, the result of a collaborative grant between the district and the city.

THE ARTS CORE

Another area featuring community integration, the Arts Core revolves around a partnership with a regional Arts-in-Education council. This permits the core to be maintained year-round and to include the entire community in its programming.

Its individuality is immediately noticed: a sloping, multi-colored two-story wall sets it apart as if something out of an animated film.

Unique here is a room two stories high, enabling uninhibited sculpturing of mammoth proportions.

Also featured: a public art gallery, "studio" classrooms and photography studios.

CENTRAL ADMINISTRATION AREA

Located immediately adjacent to the front (and the only public) entrance, the central administration area is an airy, two-story office space dominated by a winding staircase in the center and a spectacular oil-on-canvas rendition of Niagara Falls painted by prominent local artist Poll King (mother of former board president Don).

The first floor is clearly a working area — open and roomy. Telephones are available for students use; school secretaries have their work spaces here, and are able to greet guests as they arrive.

Mike Kurilovitch

The upper area consists of private offices for the executive principal and counselors.

THE COMMEMORATIVE WALK

Another unique, though easily overlooked detail is the Commemorative Walkway. It was designed to allow the community an opportunity to memorialize friends, relatives, clubs, teams and businesses by purchasing personalized markers on a special walkway.

A fund-raising initiative, the 12-by-12 inch pavers sold for $150 and included three lines of engraving. The walkway was designed as a courtyard area, boasting trees, flower planters, picnic tables and benches alongside the remembrance markers as a way of "tying the past to the future," explains Granto as he catches up with the virtual tour.

Community members past and present were invited to record their own little piece of history, to be preserved for posterity's sake alongside the history-making school.

Along the same lines, several trees that had been dedicated in memory of past students at LaSalle Senior were moved to the site of the new school in order to rightfully honor their memory.

OUTDOOR ATHLETIC FACILITIES/PARKING

In areas of the 79-acre campus where the presence of underground conduits precluded digging and/or major construction, parking lots and athletic fields were erected.

Sporting facilities include a 400-meter, all-weather track, two baseball fields, two softball fields, four soccer/lacrosse fields, and a lighted Little League football field complete with bleachers, concession stands and maintenance and storage rooms. The main fields feature irrigation and underdrain systems.

Almost 10 full acres are devoted to parking, with spaces for 775 cars and 50 buses.

"We (were) pleased to help provide Niagara Falls with modern recreational facilities at Hyde Park as part of the new high school project," said C.D. "Rapp" Rappleyea, Power Authority chairman and chief executive officer.

SAL MAGLIE STADIUM

The new, vastly improved Sal Maglie Stadium became the official home of NFHS Wolverines football and baseball as a result of the school project. A much more representative facility to honor the former Major League star than the former World War II-era public works project, its new "L' shaped design nearly doubled the former seating capacity of about 2,000 — and sat those folks considerably more comfortably, at that.

Considering that the original had been built in 1936 — and was renamed in 1983 in honor of the Falls' legendary major league pitcher (New York Giants, Brooklyn Dodgers, St. Louis Cardinals) who died in 1992 — there was plenty of modernization necessary.

Visiting team locker facilities and bullpens were added, restroom accommodations were significantly upgraded, handicap accessibility was improved to meet ADA compliance. The press box area was doubled in size, lighting was updated, and the orientation of the field was shifted roughly 45 degrees to improve conditions for participants.

"That was done so the sun is not in the fielders' eyes," notes Rollins, as the official virtual tour nears an end. "We made separate football and baseball facilities. You can pull the football field a lot closer to the bleachers, so you don't need binoculars just to see the game.

"We also amended the athletic turf surface to soil and sod. It's very durable and it helps assure proper drainage. It's just a really up-to-date, modern facility.

The new stadium conforms to minor league standards with new lockers, a weight room, individual cubicles, a Hall of Fame room and a press box.

Mike Kurilovitch

CONSTRUCTIVE COMMENTARY

Without going into boring technical issues (boring, at least, to anyone without a general contractor's license), the following are a few of the notable construction features of the project.

Elastomeric roofing and aluminum windows were chosen to keep the elements at bay and to conserve energy resources as best possible, longtime concerns with each of the school district's buildings.

Along the same lines, the latest temperature, lighting, security and fire alarm technologies were incorporated into the design, including some 62 closed-circuit cameras monitoring virtually every inch of the building.

The building employs steam heating because "steam heat reacts much faster in this part of the country," said Paul Schnettler, who oversees the building's operation for the school district. Boilers operate on natural gas or No. 2 heating oil. A water softening unit was added for the boilers due to the area's "hard" water. The softener "helps in maintaining the boilers and getting better efficiency," Schnettler noted.

Electric heaters are employed at entranceways and cabinet unit heaters are used to warm the stairwells.

Hillier's engineers were able to significantly downsize the building's heating and cooling systems by utilizing energy recovery systems. In this way, according to Hillier, "80 percent of energy typically wasted in providing ventilation" is instead recovered, reducing energy usage and in the process "providing humidifcation during cold, dry winter months."

But enough about technical specs. Let's get back to the people ...

HAVING THEIR SAY

District employees had plenty of say in the building's final design, from the purely aesthetic, such as flooring designs, to the practical, such as the heating system.

"The building is heated with steam," Rogers noted. "Most new buildings use hot water, but our staff was more familiar with steam. That had some pluses and minuses — but

Getting It Done

ultimately the costs are about the same, so we went with staff preference."

At staff's request, additional room was added to the lavatories "in order to permit repairs down the road," Rogers said. Custodial closets were also slightly reworked to better fit staff requirements.

"The maintenance staff had a lot of input as to design," Rogers said. "The instructional staff added its input on classrooms and programs, but that was more conceptual. They wanted areas for large-group learning, such as the amphitheater. The maintenance contributions were more concrete" in terms of actual facility.

Rogers credited Hillier with "involving all stake holders" in the design process.

"The design really was done client-based," he said. "We couldn't afford all (staff) ideas, but we incorporated as many as we could."

CHAPTER 10
ALL SAID AND DONE

Call it "Promises Delivered."

Two short years after the fact — wonderful, eventful years that saw a gala grand opening and an undefeated basketball team falling a whisker short of a state championship — the project resulting in a new Niagara Falls High School has to be considered an unqualified success.

The building itself amazes all who come to see it, be they educators, lawmakers or just plain folk curious to see the direction education is taking in the 21st century. Visitors have been many, coming from both near and far — as near as neighboring Buffalo, as far as The Netherlands — to personally view this "revolution in the making." Not one has failed to walk away completely and utterly impressed.

"The visitors from the teacher-prep college in Ohio — Antioch College — they were fascinated by it," said executive principal Mohr.

"The building itself, the way it is designed, is just amazing," commented Laurie Pferr, Albany chief of staff for Sen. George Maziarz. "The concept of a school-within-a-school is just fabulous. You have a big school, and yet it's not. It definitely exceeded my expectations."

While still too early to effectively gauge, the early returns on student outcomes have been nothing less than encouraging. Graduation rates are up, dropouts are down. Suspensions for aggressive behavior reduced a remarkable 33 percent in just one year.

"That doesn't happen just because you put kids in a new building," notes Mohr. "There were a lot of things we did to achieve that: security measures, diversity training for the staff and kids."

Those concerns over the violence likely from mixing two rival populations? Never materialized.

"The community had a real perception of discipline problems arising from combining the populations," Mohr said, "but not one problem that we were aware of was a result of that. Not one."

What's more, vandalism has been a virtual non-issue, and concerns over those school-issued laptops proved largely baseless. Fewer than 25 out of some 2,400 were reported stolen in the first year — a meager one percent, a rate which Granto rightfully noted was significantly lower than the local quota for car thefts.

Damage resulting from irresponsible care was a bigger concern, prompting a panel to recommend that parents of students with damaged computers foot the costs for repair — or else forfeit future usage.

Regardless, Mohr said, whether the problem was damage, theft (entire units as well as expensive parts) or loss, they were problems with which countless other school districts would dearly love to be saddled.

"We've had feedback from all over New York State, the United States and Europe," Mohr said. "They are envious of the problems we are having in terms of the technology. They would love to be in the same boat. That technology is truly one of the fundamental ways in which we are changing education."

Mohr said that regardless of the reason for a particular group's visit — whether to learn more of the creative financing end, the innovative programming or the "school-within-a-school" concept — attention invariably focuses upon the technology.

"Even with Utica, which is looking to combine (schools) and was interested in the financing," Mohr said. "They always bring a 'techie' to see why we did what we did. We not only leveled the playing field, we raised it to another level, and now other districts are trying to catch up. That showed great foresight on the part of the district."

It also showed a tremendous amount of faith in those students.

"All of a sudden they had a new lease on what it all means," said Laurie Pferr from Sen. Maziarz's office. "They were being trusted with equipment — computers. That means a lot in telling kids you are somebody."

It would also seem to go a long way toward confirming Granto's hypothesis that atmosphere and physical setting do, indeed, affect academic achievement.

"You can see it already in the attitude of the kids," Granto said. "Attendance is up. It's no longer cool to mess with each other.

"You can see it in the pride they take in their laptops. They feel good about themselves, which is a key. When you don't have something, you begin to feel that what others are saying about you is true. It becomes a self-fulfilling prophecy. This all breaks that cycle. They are discovering they can do lots of things. All this should lead to better results."

While teachers — and the district — expect more from students, they in turn expect more from their instructors.

"And that's good to see," Granto said.

The district, in turn, demanded much from its employees, what with the increased emphasis on "teaming," not to mention the shift toward more technologically advanced classrooms.

"Staff-wise, the change was more difficult," Mohr said. "Some people love change, the greatest majority are in the middle, and on the lower end there were some whose whole world was upended, who had to change things they'd been doing for years."

Things like dittos and supplemental books? Obsolete, thanks to technology.

"There are other ways to do that now," as Mohr noted.

Despite the upheaval, and the stubborn reluctance of some to embrace the technology and enter the 21st century, the change had to be viewed as overwhelmingly positive.

"For the most part the staff has been incredible," Mohr said. "For some it was difficult. But as far as the facility — my God. The people coming from the former Niagara Falls High School felt they had died and gone to heaven. Heat, light, no water dripping ... even parking."

But the new Niagara Falls High isn't about the teachers and their lifestyles as much as it is about the young adults they teach and the lives they are shaping.

They latched onto that technology like a lifeline. Sure, there were some "acceptable use" issues — a verbiage change has now put more teeth into the policy governing such use — but in the final analysis, the move undeniably helped to better prepare them for the world in which they will live and work.

So much so, in fact, that many graduating seniors inquired about purchasing the laptops to which they had become accustomed.

"They said they would be lost in college without it," Mohr said. Such arrangements are being considered for down the road.

THE MORE, THE MERRIER

Still not convinced? Need more proof that the new Niagara Falls High School sits squarely on the cutting edge? How about this — in its first year, the school district had about 200 unexpected registrants. The following year, nearly 300 more signed up to attend. Some are parochial school transfers, but many are out-of-district kids (including at least one Canadian citizen) paying tuition to attend NFHS. Some even came over from suburban Lewiston-Porter, traditionally one of the highest-rated public high schools in Western New York.

"In the past you rarely, if ever, saw anyone come here specifically to attend the old Niagara Falls High School or LaSalle," Mohr noted. "But there has been great attention to this building."

Community agencies have bought in; among those currently partnering with the school are the United Way, Youth Court, Hospice, Niagara County Probation, Family and Children's Services, Beeman Clinic (a youth and family counseling program) and Opportunities Unlimited (a program for mentally and physically handicapped adults).

Perhaps most importantly, however, the community itself has come to embrace the building as its own. Recreational swimmers fill the pool during the summer, the health-conscious take to the indoor track, senior citizens line up for introductory computer courses. The auditorium has been booked on a regular basis for everything from theatrical shows to seminars. And that's just the beginning.

Granto's efforts toward consensus-building have resulted in beneficial partnerships previously unseen, pairings sure to enhance the educational environment in the future.

That hoped-for spark, the dreams that the new school would serve as the catalyst for future growth? Evidence is beginning to mount that those wishful "pie-in-the-sky'ers" may have been right after all.

"We've come to envision schools as educational centers of our communities," commented Debra Colley, Ph.D., dean of the Niagara University College of Education, "and you have much wider input now: parents, businesses. I see that not only as the school giving to the community, but the community giving to the school. And I see that as part of revitalization efforts.

"This school has become the hub of the community ... a civic center, an arts center, a place to hold events and business meetings. It's more than just an 8-to-3 school program."

By bringing businesses, schools and the community together at the same table, Granto fostered an environment that ""brings life to everything happening in the community," Colley said.

"Carmen Granto did all the little things right," she said. "He created consensus that gave the people ownership. He had everything lined up. This school is a critical piece for Niagara Falls. It's not just a building, but a component for creating a place where people will move — businesses, families, everyone.

"Excellent schools draw families, and I believe you do see that starting to happen in Niagara Falls," Colley said. "Niagara University recently hired a number of faculty, and they didn't look at us, they looked at the schools in the community. The higher the standards and the more that school is promoted, the more you'll have families moving into that community. It won't happen overnight ... but there is a lot of evidence showing that schools have revitalized communities."

The community? Well, it benefited in ways too numerous to count.

Not only did it receive an incredible new facility — gift-wrapped — there were significant improvements to infrastructure and enhancements to recreational facilities. The city ice rink was restored, its stadium rebuilt. The working relationship between the school board and the City Council was bolstered. Residents were energized.

Oh yeah, and it all happened without any negative impact on the tax rates.

By the way, the city also gained a much-needed cultural center as a direct byproduct of the school project. The "old" Niagara Falls High — at first slated to meet the wrecking ball in favor of a commercial project — was saved from that rather ignoble plight by a plucky group of local preservationists.

Bolstered by a community not wishing to lose yet another of its landmark structures, the group convinced the city to take ownership of the building and has worked diligently to find tenants for what has since been renamed the "Niagara Arts and Cultural Center."

The grass-roots effort included a volunteer drive to assist with clean up of the building. Several local artists have found — to their delight — that the building offers hard-to-find affordable studio space, all in an atmosphere that promotes interaction amongst the craftsmen.

Talking-stage plans included discussions for a rooftop restaurant, among other attractions. While that has yet to materialize, other impressive ventures have.

Even that updated Sal Maglie Stadium harbors new promise for the city and the community: with its impressive improvements, it may provide the impetus to help bring minor league baseball back to the Falls after an absence of several years (the New York-Penn League and even the Buffalo Bisons formerly called the city home).

So the NFHS project, in virtually every respect, has truly been win-win. Or, more appropriately, win-win-win-win-win.

A classic example of big-league thinking in what, for far too many years, had been a bush-league town.

Those directly involved with the project sing its praises at every opportunity.

"It worked out just fantastic," said Hillier principal-in-charge David Chase. "It was very highly organized: regular team meetings, an action plan, schedules. It was a case of laying out a plan and accomplishing it, piece by piece.

Mike Kurilovitch

"We are a firm known for design excellence, and we saw an opportunity — with the vision of this board of education and district — to do something special, a vision for the future. The client was open to new ideas" in terms of such traditionally sacred — and as such, "untouchable" — aspects as facility and scheduling.

The result was a school building — and it seems woefully inadequate to describe it so simply — that redefines schools.

"I would love to have other opportunities (like this), but they are rare," Chase said. "These don't come along every day and that's why we jumped on it. This was a wonderful experience. We have developed bonds with the people in Niagara Falls that will go on beyond the project. This was just a moment in time ... something special. I feel we have made a real contribution to education, and certainly to Niagara Falls."

Hillier has moved on, of course, and at last glance was doing school work in seven other East Coast states. In retrospect, Chase said that the overtime required for the Niagara Falls project "hurt the bottom line for us, but that was a minor issue. We felt it was an investment for our future. We wanted to be part of the Honeywell-Niagara Falls team, and it worked out just fantastic."

Leadership and cooperation were the key elements in achieving what Chase termed "our best (work) to date, no question."

"It was a special setting, an experiment with something outside-the-box. This (project) was set up as a skunk works, as a Beta test to see if this type of collaboration makes a difference — and it does," Chase said. "The district professionals, the state, the labor unions, contractors, subcontractors, everyone ... the cooperation was the key. You sit at a table when there is a problem and everyone wants to solve it, rather than just protect themselves. We all had the same goal.

"Most of the time you have a boat with oars being pulled in different directions," Chase said. "But these people knew where they wanted to go. It all goes back to the attitude of cultural leadership existing even before we came on board — instead of 'let's get it done as best we can' it was 'how do we get it done?'

"I hope this is the trend for the future," Chase said. "This was easy."

Well, maybe not exactly easy ...

"We were over budget several times and had to come back," Chase said. "There are always compromises that occur — the pool was in and out and then back in, but at a reduced size — but the quality was never compromised. The conceptual design stayed pretty much intact.

"It had been kind of known in the (architectural) world that there were problems with the project in the early stages," Chase said. "Given the same circumstances in other settings, it wouldn't have been as successful. But this board president (King) and the board of education itself and the superintendent were all on the same page. That's leadership, and that is special.

"We have done work with many, many clients who, although interested in designing a building for the future, ultimately lack the courage or the support to get there. This superintendent and school board had the courage, desire and attitude for this project to succeed. It was win-win-win for the district, the children and the city."

Chase singled out Luaces for possessing the "creative spark to make it happen."

"He went far beyond the call of duty. He gave up personal time, weekends and so on," Chase said, "and it was because Jorge had ownership of the project in his mind. He deserves yeoman's credit. He's our star designer, he was asked and he said he would do it. He recognized the opportunity for working with a superior collaborative group."

The work Luaces and Co. did in less than five months' time "usually would have taken 12 months," Chase said.

"That ownership attitude is a real key," he added. "You make sacrifices and set priorities based on your own agenda."

As for Luaces, NFHS represented his personal Sistine Chapel.

"I would have to categorize this as the most successful school project I have ever worked on," he said. "I'm a big supporter of that team there. They are second to none." Even the time issue worked out OK in the end, he said, triggering "a lot of fast, excellent thinking."

Right down to the peripherals — the community improvements, the new sports and recreational facilities — people are impressed. The Little League football moms are thrilled with their new digs; even Ice Pavilion patrons were impressed with the upgrades to that facility.

As a school, the project has delivered everything promised, and then some. As a community center, it has triggered a rejuvenation of the arts and has played host to countless events.

COME TOGETHER, RIGHT NOW — OVER ME

In terms of uniting the community, the early returns are encouraging.

"Hopefully it brings the people together," Senator Maziarz said. "When you consolidate two schools there will inevitably be some growing pains, but I'm hoping that eventually it marks the beginning of Niagara Falls coming together, and that it allows the people of the western end of Niagara County to see what they're capable of doing. You have to start that changing of attitudes with these kinds of things."

In terms of providing an economic stimulus, of fueling a rebirth, the jury is still out, but the outlook is certainly encouraging.

The final word, however, rests with the youth of Niagara Falls. It will be spoken in volumes, not in how they talk about the building, but in how they treat it.

"I really hope the kids attending will respect that school," Assemblywoman Delmonte said. "That wonderful pool, the library, all that wonderful natural light ... I would feel very fortunate as a student attending that building. I would say 'thank you for giving me this.'

"I know it's just a building, but it's a building that came with a lot of forethought, a lot of caring, to make it the best it could be. It has all the niceties and amenities, things a lot of other schools don't have. I will feel very sad if it is defaced, if the kids don't give it the respect it's due. I hope they enjoy it and utilize it."

She anticipates the same spirit of pride and cooperation from the citizenry.

"That goes for the community, as well. It's not a closed facility. It is a community asset. I hope the community members, once they see it for what it is, will really appreciate it. It took a lot of work to get it to where it is."

Basking in a well-earned retirement, Pillittere thinks back on the NFHS project with pride.

He said that gaining passage of the legislation allowing the one-of-a-kind project to proceed was among his most gratifying accomplishments in elected office.

"It ranks second to my Right To Know bill of 1980," which dealt with exposure to toxins in the workplace. "That (legislation) entailed a similar type of struggle," Pillittere said. "Big business was opposed; they felt we were preventing workers from working. They were concerned with protecting secret formulas and recipes.

"Half the legislators hated (the bill), half loved it. The Senate hated it. They thought it was anti-business and would cost jobs. The Assembly felt too many workers were being killed. It was a brand-new concept, the same type of legislation" that ultimately created the school.

Pillittere also hopes that Niagarans recognize what they have been given.

"This gives kids a better environment in which to learn," he said. "In a way it's isolated," so the focus can be entirely upon education.

"It's a beautiful facility," Pillittere said. "As soon as the kids walk in their minds should be ready for learning."

"I am very proud to have been involved with the legislation that allowed Niagara Falls to build this school," said former state senator, now Buffalo comptroller Anthony Nanula. "This is a model not only for this area, but for the entire country. I'm very proud we did it in Niagara Falls."

Said DiFrancesco: "We left a culture, we left 112 years of history when we left that old building. But that was yesterday for our graduates. This is tomorrow for our kids."

Mike Kurilovitch

THE SINCEREST FORM OF FLATTERY

The final word on the subject belongs to the Buffalo City School District, keepers of the state's oldest collection of school buildings. Currently planning a staggering $971 million school renovation project — patterned directly after the successful Niagara Falls venture — the district is looking to the experts.

Chosen from four finalists to perform the top-to-bottom rehabilitation of some 64 schools was a contingent headed by one Carmen Granto of Niagara Falls, New York.

Other key members of the team: Buffalo's own Ciminelli Construction, the Hillier Architectural Group and organizational mastermind Steve Rollins.

Buffalo Mayor Anthony Masiello noted that the project will "touch children in every neighborhood and create lasting value throughout the city from the spinoff of jobs, training and new business."

Sound familiar?

Equating the venture to the massive power plant construction in Lewiston back in the late '50s and early '60s, Douglas Francis, executive director of the Joint Schools Construction Board, noted that "Robert Moses (was) the last person (to be) in charge of a project of these proportions."

Ciminelli's Giardino, underscored the gravity of such a plan when he summed up his group's interest: "This is our city. We live here. We raise our families here, and we think this project holds out the opportunity for fundamental change across the entire community.

"At the end of the day, we want people to say 'I moved to the City of Buffalo because of the quality of the schools'."

Buffalo-Niagara, Niagara-Buffalo. Forever linked in educational excellence.

For more information on the Niagara Falls High School project, or to view additional project plans and photographs, visit the Niagara Falls City School District website at http://www.nfschools.net.

CHAPTER 11
ODDS AND ENDS

There's certainly no shortage of opinions when it comes to Niagara Falls, its people and politics and, of course, the new Niagara Falls High School. What follows, then, is a selection of sentiments from those who know the project most intimately, arranged topically.

Of course, **the politically charged atmosphere that is Niagara County and Niagara Falls** was, to put it mildly, a central issue for many of the participants. Here's what a couple of them thought, in typically candid fashion:

STEVE ROLLINS: "It's a very difficult environment up here. The City of Niagara Falls has been very difficult to work with ... I don't believe it's personal, it's just a lack of decision-makers taking responsibility. They cleverly defer a lot of the process. Fortunately we had very few dealings with the city. Most that we had were not very good.

"Then there's the unions — that's historical. It's a tough union environment here. There's equipment sabotage, disagreements ... We had a guaranteed no-strike clause in the contract, but I guess they forgot to negotiate a no-sick clause. I guess guys must have all got something bad for lunch one day."

As for who should take responsibility for the anti-development attitude so prevalent in the area, Rollins said there's plenty of blame to spread around.

"Everyone is responsible — unions, government, labor costs ... the labor contracts are prohibitive. You have some real tough challenges here. Some tough decisions need to be made, but they just can't get out of their own way. This area could be so much ... it is such beautiful country up here. There's a lot of history here. Good Lord — how much more historical can you get than this? But you drive down Main Street and all you see is plywood over doors and windows. They can't see the forest for the trees. They are their own worst enemy. I don't blame it all on Niagara County. Albany hasn't done anything for Niagara County or Western New York at all. They're all ignored by

Albany. Thank God for the school district — if not for them, there would be no renewal here."

DON KING agreed, saying that the prevailing political climate in the Falls would have dealt a lethal blow to less-determined groups.

"Something like this is very difficult to do via political avenues, with all the governmental politics, especially in the area we're in — Western New York, Niagara Falls, the Northeast United States."

In spite of it all, ROLLINS found **trust and cooperation** where it was needed most: On the part of the school board.

"The district didn't know me from the man on the moon when I first came on board, but they came to trust me to look out for their interests. The relationship has been so rewarding. I was able to be so much more effective because they trusted me.

"That's uncommon for Niagara County, the way business is done here, to embrace an outsider like me — to make decisions on their behalf, to speak on their behalf. Niagara County is full of mistrust. No one trusts anyone around here. I was able to bring all my years of experience in this business, and the true value of that, to the table, because I was trusted. There was a great deal of mutual respect in that regard. That's not to say that there weren't moments ... it wasn't all 'yes sir, no sir,' the slap-on-the-back, good-buddies thing. It was like a marriage. We quarreled, but it was never personal — just business. And you win some, you lose some."

Said MIKE REDMOND, former business manager for Plumbers and Steam fitters Local 22: "It worked well here. Would it work elsewhere? Maybe not. You'd need the cooperation of all parties involved. If they're not willing to work (together), it won't work. Without total cooperation you will run into massive roadblocks."

As long as we're on the subject of politically (incorrect) speaking, you can always count on Falls school board member MARK ZITO to be controversial. And he was at his confrontational best in confronting those who stubbornly sought to undermine the high school project because they didn't want to see the old building closed or, worse yet, razed.

Getting It Done

Speaking to the **community's zeal to maintain its old school buildings**, Zito said the key to the solution is boiling away all the emotional factors and reducing the "broth" to dollars and cents — make that "sense."

"I don't know whether many communities have assessed the age and condition of their buildings versus (the cost of) replacing them, but when you take into consideration (the expense involved in) wiring them for technology and so on ... frequently the costs far outweigh the value to the community.

"People are (turning) high schools into monuments, while not allowing for the business sense of it. They think that by knocking down a community's high school you're knocking down its realities, its dreams. That building becomes a symbol for all that has happened. In reality, any business would have dumped that structure a long time ago."

The man, the myth, the legend: Few of those having any connection to the school project could resist giving their impressions of **Carmen Granto and his role in the proceedings.**

ROBERT BENNETT of the New York State Board of Regents, calling Granto "one of the finest school leaders in the nation," proceeded to praise his tenacity with the project.

"School leadership is not easy these days," he said. "He has exemplified great integrity and risk-taking, and look at the result."

ROLLINS, on Granto: "This project was tremendously successful because of one person — Carmen Granto. If it weren't for him, this project wouldn't be where it is. You wouldn't have the building, you wouldn't have the success. His decision making and willingness to accept responsibility for making decisions was absolutely key to getting things done. In a project like this you need that.

"He would defer to committees for their experience, knowledge and input. We needed a strong decision maker and his decisions were always decisive and timely. Only because of that did we get through the design process in five and-a-half months. That was an unbelievable hurdle. He was right there all the way, on the front line. How he did that — which was a full-time job — and still ran the school system, is a testament to the man. I have a tremendous amount of respect for him. He always challenges people to do more with less and to overachieve. He's a leader by example."

Executive principal PHILIP MOHR: "This is Carmen Granto's legacy. He has truly been the heart and guts of making this change — the funding, the grandiose look, involving stake holders, not raising taxes. He really has done something here that is very, very unique, and I attribute that to his drive and vision. In a community striving for some economic stability and jobs, that is all the more amazing."

GRANTO on Granto, and on his recipe for success: "Every day you've got to watch a variety of things: The political and private climate to make sure that it stays positive, that no fiefdoms develop, no infighting; you have to make sure the elected officials are happy, that the unions get what they have coming, that the contractors aren't gouging you.

"You have to keep at it every day. It becomes your job, not a thing you do in addition to your job."

What company could have resisted involvement in such a ground-breaking undertaking? Certainly not Ciminelli. JOHN GIARDINO, on **his company's interest in the project**: "What attracted our company was the vision of the project itself. You had a community led by a superintendent with an acute awareness of its needs, and they found very unconventional ways to address those needs.

"The design was unique and purposeful, it's a great facility, it was clearly an outstanding project which we very much wanted to be involved in. Every day there were a lot of unknowns for everyone, and unless there was a feeling of trust with everyone, it never would have gotten done."

DON KING on **the importance of the school board president to such a project**: "I kept the stamina up so the whole thing didn't get derailed by the community. A key thing the board did was letting the superintendent and his staff do their jobs. The newspaper was against us at the time; we'd lost a couple of board members with longevity because they were in favor of the high school" and were not reelected.

"Board members are very vulnerable," King said. "My greatest input was trying to keep the board stabilized, with the

Getting It Done

negative community attitude and objections from a lot of parents. And there's no tougher obstacle than resistance by the media.

"I knew we were right, as I look back," King said. "We focused on what was in the best interest of all kids. Looking back now, the kids are better served and it happened without raising taxes, not at all."

KING again, on the **site selection**: "The Hyde Park site wasn't necessarily my first choice — although Hyde Park is one of the jewels of the community, and this should complement it.

"If the community had been willing to think of the greater Niagara area as a unit, instead of pockets," the DeVeaux site would have been the natural choice, he said.

"Overlooking the gorge, all that land, the scenery, making it an international school," he said, ticking off its assets. "We could have put up a hotel at the site, run by students.

"My second choice was something in the center of the city."

ROY ROGERS: "Our preference was the DeVeaux site, but community reaction and price shot that down. This (Hyde Park) site is more centrally located, and when the board of education decided to consolidate, it made the most sense to go to Hyde Park. We actually had looked at that site at one time and discounted it, because we knew the (conduits) were underneath."

KING one more time, on **the decision to close the two high schools**: "It wasn't as tough as closing some neighborhood schools. Those high schools really weren't (neighborhood schools), so to speak, so bringing them together was really the right thing to do. Seeing this changing community — the demographics — combining the two schools wasn't a tough decision for me at all."

MOHR on **the district's initiatives to keep the new school safe and orderly**: "We have moved very swiftly and appropriately with rules infringements. Mess up and you're out. I have to pat Carmen Granto and the board of education on the back for that. They haven't flinched on it. If you want to set a culture, you have to know what you want it to look like. You're not going to bring your problems from the street into this building. That's not going to fly here.

Mike Kurilovitch

"It's kind of like what the suburbs have done for years. Have a central location, bus everyone in and you don't have that constant parade of street issues coming into the building."

MIKE REDMOND on **why he bought into the project despite its initial disfavor amongst unions**: "The old high school was a wreck. It was beyond the ability to repair, believe me. So knowing everything involved, being a resident, knowing the need for a new high school, I agreed to it. I don't know if I would do it again. The people we worked with were extremely honorable (the school district and Honeywell) and everything worked out to my satisfaction."

Ironically, Redmond believed that a public referendum to bond the proposed project "never would have passed here," which would have meant no new school for Niagara Falls.

AND KING once more, this time on **the key to accomplishing the project** at all — a move the board had made years before, signing and then keeping Granto in the fold: "Maintaining that stability is crucial," he said. "The average superintendent's tenure is three years. Boards change. Without the stability and trust between the superintendent and the board, this couldn't have happened."

ROBERT DiFRANCESCO on **saying goodbye to the former Niagara Falls High after 112 years**: "By pooling our resources in one place we were able to offer things no one anywhere has. With one school there was no more divisiveness ... it was cost-effective, no more duplicity. And the youngsters came together beautifully — we never saw so much as a hint of this awful blood-hate supposedly existing between the two high schools. We did very well bringing the two cultures of students, faculties and families together.

"If we hadn't done it this way we wouldn't have this beautiful place — we'd still be in that hole, where everything was breaking down terribly. We couldn't have gone two more years there. I love that old barn on Pine and Portage, but we left that behind. We said 'goodbye' at a strawberries-and-champagne breakfast at the old school ... That was yesterday for our graduates; this is tomorrow for our kids. We knew it was time. They have a better opportunity here in the long run, and we're trying to do what's right for our kids in the long run."

Getting It Done

AMERICAN SCHOOL AND UNIVERSITY magazine hailed the project's potential in terms of **focusing education resources on the business of learning, rather than building**.

"This may be a way for school districts to act as any other tenant," the magazine wrote, a move that could "funnel money back to academic programs instead of physical facilities."

Similar arrangements are done in parts of Canada, the magazine noted, and are bound to become more commonplace as school districts scrape for ways to extend the finite amount of taxpayer dollars afforded them.

The National School Boards Association, in its "School Board News" publication, also gave the proposition its stamp of approval. It noted that traditional bonding would have ended up costing the district more after factoring in interest and debt retirement.

And the final word on the subject of **leasing and schools** belongs to the man of the hour himself, CARMEN GRANTO, as expressed in a written piece for *Scholastic Administrator*:

"How did we do all of this? By letting go of the idea of owning equipment or even buildings, and embracing the concept of leasing. Rather than raising taxes, we began to think as a business. We decided that the school district would adhere to its core business — teaching and learning — and we would partner with the private sector in innovative ways to provide our students with the very best.

All of our technology and its support systems, even our new high school, are leased. As a result, our students and community have the best and most up-to-date equipment and resources. In short, we have established powerful public-private partnerships that give our community — which typically would have no chance of competing with more affluent communities — the belief that our students can compete with everyone.

"Our city's bleeding economy was partly what drove us to consider leasing. The other was attaining equity for our students. Most of our young adults are leaving Niagara Falls. We decided if they're going to leave for better opportunities the least we could do is give them skills to compete in a high-tech job market. Plus, as we were raising academic standards for our students, we had to look at the standard of our facilities. When you have to cancel high school basketball games because it's raining in the gym, something has to change. Without many financial resources, we had to think creatively. I came up with leasing out of necessity; it was the only way we could afford to improve anything in our district.

"Indeed, leasing isn't for everyone. But it is an alternative that more cash-strapped districts are considering, or may want to consider. Any other community can do this, and make it work for them. It just takes courage and political will."

QUICK HITTERS

"The New York Power Authority has to become a much better neighbor than it has been in the past. This was a good place to start." — Senator GEORGE MAZIARZ

"We knew the people would come to the plate. We knew everyone was watching us, too. And we knew that no matter what, it would come. It was like a mission from God. We knew the old high school didn't give our kids a tomorrow. This is a whole new world." ROBERT DiFRANCESCO

"This was new ground for everyone. Were there surprises? Yes. Did it work out for everyone? Not always. But at the end of the day you look at that high school, and it's just a great place for kids to learn. You can tell there is a lot of pride in the kids who go to the school." CARMEN GRANTO

"I'm very pleased with the way it all worked out. I was curious to see whether it would come in on-time and under- or at-budget. If it had come in way over budget, then we would have had problems. As it was, to me it was a success. From the Albany perspective, the final judgment is in the financial end." MAZIARZ

"It's a big place, but I believe the kids are happy. They like coming here. The only time it seems unwieldy is at bus arrival and departure, and I attribute that to good design." MOHR

"It's nice to see something so positive come from a piece of legislation. I can remember running into (Joe) Pillittere's office many times at midnight, asking if it was going to make it through, getting pieces done in special sessions. It just seemed like we were constantly explaining, pushing, prodding, getting all the pieces in place and making sure it was technically correct." LAURIE PFERR

"The maximum price guarantee really became the lynch pin. In order to raise money through Certificates of Participation ... it was the most important element to building this school. We gave the district a guaranteed maximum price and we had to work diligently to see it could happen." JOHN GIARDINO

"We had a good job. Obviously there were no fatalities, no real serious injuries, so that always makes it a good job for us." TOM PRICE, Ironworkers union

"(The school is) a technological statement for the 21st century and a civic centerpiece for local citizens." ARCHITECTURE WEEK, August 2000

"It's been way more than I expected." Then-freshman KIMMISSIE MOORE after spending her first week in her new school.

"I got the greatest compliment I could expect from some teens who toured the building and told me the inside reminded them of a mall." Architect WALTER "MAC" RAWLEY

Mike Kurilovitch

CHAPTER 12
INDEPENDENT ANALYSIS

Even the earliest philosophers recognized the worth of a good school and a good education.

"Whoso neglects learning in his youth, Loses the past and is dead for the future." — Euripides, c. 485-406 B.C. (from Phrixus, fragment 927)

Of course, over the past 2,500 years schools have grown to represent much more than mere centers for learning. They've grown to become integral parts of our communities, hosting business meetings, cultural events, family activities, raising hopes and expectations.

"They're much more than just 8-to-3 (structures)," notes Dr. Debra Colley, Dean of the Niagara University College of Education.

"Schools become the hub of their community," Colley said. "There is much wider input now — parents, businesses. We see that as a school giving to a community and the community giving back to the school."

Because of that, schools have been recognized as critical pieces of the overall puzzle, essential to the revitalization of the communities in which they are situated.

"Especially in rural communities, there is a lot of evidence showing schools have revitalized communities,' Colley said. "They bring about new partnerships between the schools, business, the community. When you get those entities planning together it brings life to everything happening in that community. You get partnerships which didn't exist previously."

That's happening in Niagara Falls now. And it happened not a moment too soon.

"We had kind of bottomed out," Colley said. "Our airport was going nowhere, we'd almost lost our status of being a city from lost population ...(People) realized that they may not get along, but they needed to do something."

That "something" was the new high school. At the very least, Colley said, it brought much-needed attention to the area. And the attention has already spawned growth — even with the airport, now under examination for playing a much larger role in the area's future plans.

"If a school district can make that happen, they can make anything happen," Colley said. "The school is very central to all that. It renewed enthusiasm. It created a sense that we can do anything in this community because we have the right people in place."

To hope that a new Niagara Falls High School could trigger a renaissance for the Rust Belt city is not a pipe dream, she insists.

"Keep in mind that the higher the standards and the more the school is promoted, the more you will have families moving into that community" to capitalize upon the opportunity, she said. Her own Niagara University recently hired a number of faculty, she pointed out.

"And they didn't look at us so much as they looked at the schools here."

"This is a critical piece for Niagara Falls. It's not just a building, it's a component. We are creating a place where people will move (to), businesses, families, everyone. If it were just a building it would be absent of that vision. But it is a center for collaboration, the centerpiece of the community. It offers a strong, solid academic program. Make no mistake: Excellent schools draw families. And I believe I do see something starting to happen in Niagara Falls.

"It won't happen overnight," but it will happen.

Colley noted that the initial opposition to the school project was "so like Niagara, having seen past failures and not wanting to try something new."

The success of the project, she said, should open a few eyes.

"It may have made people realize that you have to give up something to create a new image."

It may even help recoup some of that population loss, so detrimental to the city over the past four decades.

""It begins with education," Colley said. "Create a prestigious, high-performing school system and people will rally around that. People check out the schools before they decide to move anywhere. Now we have something to offer them."

Folks who visit the school — as was the case with a recent NU program hosted there — invariably "walk away raving about the educational system in Niagara Falls," Colley said.

Even the kids who go there feel better about themselves and their situations as a result of the new building, she said.

"When you're in a run-down, yucky place, you feel yucky," she said. "The kids are very proud of that school. They're in a place they can be proud of, and that will definitely impact their performance. A lot of how well you do is in how well you feel you can do. Kids have demonstrated respect for what happens there ... (and that) turns the academics around pretty quickly."

As for the surrounding community, just give it some time, Colley urges.

"The full impact won't happen overnight. There remains a lot that needs to be done in Niagara Falls," she said. "But this exciting operation with the district is a pivotal piece for the community. A critical step is having the right people working together, and it is happening in Niagara Falls. We have people talking about the tough issues. They are ready to go. People have shared a goal and vision and they are all coming together to make it happen.

"The school system, with Carmen Granto's leadership showing the way, has brought together the most unexpected people. And that sets the stage for innovation and success. That sends a message that it is possible ... working together we can meet our goals."

Of course, academic improvement has to be the bottom line. All the resources and facilities combined won't mean a thing if kids are still failing.

Success stories are necessary in order to energize Niagara's stock.

"The ones going off and bringing notoriety to the area — the success stories — that's what will result in people staying here and raising families here," Colley said. "The kids will be the ones leading the way. We're turning out wonderful young

Getting It Done

people, well-prepared. They are leaders, and that's what brings people back into the city."

The "new" Niagara Falls High School will play a tremendous part in making that happen. And it is all possible — everything — only because the project was done properly, with forethought and vision, from the outset.

"Carmen Granto did all the things right," Colley said. "He created consensus, he gave ownership, he had everything lined up.

"The district had no reputation before. Now they have created a cutting edge school and program, and everyone is interested in seeing how it happened. Success breeds success."

As a parting thought, consider this from John Ruskin, from "Unto The Last," composed in 1862:

"Let us reform our schools, and we shall find little reform needed in our prisons."

Amen.

Mike Kurilovitch

EPILOGUE

Dr. Lawrence Lezotte

During the 1989-90 school year, I was contracted by the New York Department of Education to present workshops on our Effective Schools Research throughout the state. It was then that the Niagara Falls School District first invited me to deliver the same message to all its administrators and teachers. From that time on, I worked intermittently with the school district to provide training and technical assistance as it reformed its schools.

It was my privilege to work with hundreds of school districts throughout the United States over the last decade or so. Niagara Falls was one of a relatively small number of districts that was serious about school reform, and persisted its efforts to provide each student with a quality education. I often cite Niagara Falls as being one of my best students. The teachers, administrators, and board members deserve the credit for the hard work that went into making it a good school system. I know they share my view that while the progress to date deserves to be celebrated, school effectiveness in Niagara Falls remains a work in progress.

Those involved in the new high school project from the outset know that the Niagara Falls Board of Education, and Superintendent Granto, insisted that the new school be more than a new building in which the same old work occurred. They recognized that a change of physical location was no guarantee that the philosophy, core values, and approaches to teaching and learning would reflect the best practice without careful planning and hard work. To that end, the joint quality councils from the existing high schools were empowered to assume leadership for reinventing and renewing the instructional program and collateral services that would operate in the new school.

Many of the administrators from the District felt that, as an outsider with some established credibility in the system, I could play a facilitating role in helping the joint quality councils to think outside the box. I was asked to meet with the quality councils one or two days every other month, and did so, for over two years.

What was your initial charge and did it change over time?

Initially, I saw my role as an information-giver. In that regard, I tried to bring relevant research to the discussions. I hoped it would provide the basis for planning the new program that would be launched with the opening of the new school. As time passed, I feel that my role did change from information-giver to more of a problem-solver and provocateur.

One of the first and most important tasks that the joint quality councils had to complete was reaching consensus on the mission, core beliefs, and values that would create the focus for all subsequent decisions. In addition to reaching consensus, the joint quality council members had to get their constituencies back home to endorse the mission, core beliefs, and core values. It would have been a hollow victory if only the council members subscribed to them. In seeking endorsement, the council members emphasized that, once accepted, the mission and belief statements would serve as the basis for all subsequent decision-making regarding programs, resource allocations, and staff needs, to mention but a few areas. In other words, this was of the highest priority and everyone had a vested interest.

Besides assisting here and there with issues of wording, editorial refinements, and clarity, I attempted to mediate compromises where needed. As a dispassionate outsider, I was able to intervene from time to time.

Once the stake holder communities adopted the mission and beliefs, the joint quality councils turned their attention to developing goals and action plans designed to bring the mission to life. At this point, it was helpful for the work teams to look at research and proven practices as a source of guidance. I feel I helped to provide some direction for this massive effort and, as a result, the committees covered a tremendous amount of material in a relatively short time.

The action teams then returned to the joint quality councils with their recommendations. Along with others, I asked how this or that recommendation, or strategy, fit the mission and core values. This was not an easy task. By that time, those who made the recommendations had a great deal invested in their work. It was necessary to challenge the work without challenging the people. I learned a lot from this process. In Niagara Falls, I saw for myself that dedicated and caring people can disagree without becoming disagreeable. This factor may be as important as anything else in predicting that the mission, beliefs, and action steps will be implemented and sustained in the new school.

What was your ultimate role and how would you assess the impact on the overall project?

I believe I described my role in the statements above. I leave it to others to explain how they viewed my role and to be the final judges of the value I added to the realization of this ambitious project. It is important to remember that the real work, reflected in the plan for the new Niagara Falls High School, was done by those involved on the joint councils and by the many other volunteers who assisted on the action teams.

At the risk of sounding self-serving, I would say to any community or school board taking on such a project in the future that there is a role for the outsider. As an outsider with some credibility, I believe that I was able to ask questions, raise issues, and point out conflicts in philosophy without getting personal. When work teams are formed in an organization, the members are chosen from a larger organizational context. The work team does not work in a vacuum and must face the others in that larger setting all the time. Sometimes people are unwilling to raise issues, or challenge others, because they know that they have to work with them tomorrow. An outsider is in a better position to raise questions and pose challenges.

I want to make one last observation about impact. As I mentioned earlier, I travel all over the country to work with numerous school districts. I have already told hundreds, if not thousands, of educators that they should look to the processes used by Niagara Falls as a way of building ownership and commitment to collaborative decision making. Niagara Falls, and the processes that were used, is already having a profound

Getting It Done

impact on other districts and educational leaders. I am sure the district will receive visitors, and requests for information, for years to come.

Why was it (is it) important to rethink the programs along with the new building?

If we back-up from the Niagara Falls project per se, we see that expectations have changed so old programs are no longer adequate. The call for school reform has gone out across the United States generally, and in New York specifically. The programs of every high school, new and old, have to be rethought. In New York, the state's secondary schools were never designed for all students to meet the Board of Regents diploma requirements. The very mission of the high schools in New York changed because of new state policies. In addition, recent school and classroom research reveals that some practices, instructional strategies, and organizational structures work better than others when it comes to student learning. To sum up, even without the new physical plant, the secondary program had to be redesigned to meet the expectations of the 21st century.

The fact that the new physical plant was being planned, and subsequently built, made it easier to initiate the dialogue on program change. There were reasons for this. First, it is difficult for people to see that change is possible if the physical environment remains unchanged. Changes in the physical setting provide visible and tangible proof that there will be a new beginning. Second, the new physical structure contains many new features. Extensive technology and connectivity, for example, did not exist prior to the new school. The question of how to capitalize on these new opportunities, and incorporate them into the school operations and school culture, would have presented itself in any case. My thought, shared by the board and superintendent, was why not start the conversation from ground zero, like the school itself, and reinvent the program? In so doing, there is the opportunity to keep what you want, abandon what you do not want, and modify the rest to fit the current setting.

Although many may disagree with my views, I believe it was easier to rethink the programs because two long-standing schools were to become one. Neither LaSalle nor Niagara Falls High School could import its culture and programs and impose them on the other. Compromise and accommodation had to occur. Each school had the opportunity to bring some part of its valued culture with it, but each had to make some room for the other. If we were just closing an old school and moving that school to a new physical plant, it would have been much harder to get the leadership groups to examine questions such as: What do we care about most? What should we do to assure that all our students are able to meet the standards?

What message would have been sent if we had a state-of-the art building and an old program?

Given the larger context of educational reform, to bring an old program to a state-of-the-art building would have been a tragedy, a huge missed opportunity. The students and the community would have every right to be disappointed. They would be justified in claiming that nothing changed but the building.

An old program in a new setting would have been described by many as an expensive example of change without real difference. I believe we are at the threshold of a real program and physical change. In time, we will know whether or not all the hopes and dreams embedded in the action plans will come to pass. I am confident that real change is in those plans, but there will be tremendous pressure to do things as we have always done them.

What needed to be done differently and why?

To understand what needed to change, one must understand the changing mission of secondary education, especially the implications of the changing mission on secondary school structures, systems, and approaches to teaching and learning. When high school education was the terminal formal education experience for the vast majority of students, the primary mission was to sort and select students. To wit, high schools were supposed to find the next generation of doctors, lawyers, and garbage collectors, and move them on to their respective destinies. In those days, the school placed students on college preparatory or vocational tracks, and the students were free to learn or not. In that sense, high schools placed students in a course of study, and curriculum was served up to them cafeteria style. Since World War II, the world has changed.

First of all, high school is not now, and never again will be, the terminal formal education experience for the overwhelming majority of students. For example, 70% of all new jobs will require some education beyond high school. If we believe that, one of the most important functions of any level of K-12 schooling is to prepare students for success at the next level. If we recognize that 80 to 90% of the graduates will receive additional formal education, then we realize that high school should no longer be the sorting machine it once was. It must transform itself into a learning machine.

To emphasize this fact, virtually all states, including New York, now have accountability systems that hold schools accountable for learning, not sorting. What needs to change to transform the high school from a sorting to a learning machine? Obviously, this is a huge question and worthy of an entire book itself. Nevertheless, I will attempt to give a short answer to the question.

Sorting is something schools did to students, perhaps against their will in some cases. By contrast, learning is not something you do to someone. Virtually all learning requires not only the permission but also the active participation of the learner. Think about it this way. Learning is the product for which the school is being held accountable. The student is the final worker in the production process. If the front line worker does not do his or her work, learning will not be produced. Therefore, in order to produce the highest quality and quantity of learning, you must know what motivates students to learn at the highest possible levels.

Some of the factors that take on added significance in a learning-centered school include: 1. The relevance of the learning as perceived by the learner; 2. The extent to which there are choices and options; 3. The extent to which the learner has the prerequisite knowledge to learn; and, perhaps as important as the previous three, 4. The time to learn. The approved action plans, and the various strategies contained in them, address many of these issues. When they are finally implemented, the school will move toward the learning machine.

What were the major obstacles which had to be overcome?

This is any easy question to answer: inertia. The basic tendency of both individuals and organizations is to follow the path of least resistance, and do again what they have always done in the way they have always done it. This is equally true of schools and educators. Add to the inertia problem the fact that many parents want schools to be just like they were when they were in school, and you have a system that is difficult to change.

We noted above that virtually all learning is an act of choice on the part of the learner. We should also add the corollary that virtually all system change requires the permission and active commitment of those who maintain the status quo. Fortunately, we know something about how to create and sustain such changes. Our knowledge base of systemic and individual change is far from complete, and our track record on sustainable change is not good. Nevertheless, the processes that were used in the Niagara Falls High School project reflected the best we know how to do.

For example, we recognized the importance of stake holder involvement, since the kind of changes required in the new school could not be mandated. Change is easier, and more likely to succeed, when people understand why it is needed. For my part, I tried to take great care to explain why this or that change was needed, given the learning mission of the school. Change is more likely to occur, and be sustained, when the change effort is a group effort and when the group shares the commitment to the change. All the recommended changes have a constituency and an advocacy group. Eventually, accountability for seeing that the changes have occurred is necessary. The action plans specify times and responsibilities.

Getting It Done

My greatest fear is that too many people will see the completion of the physical plant of the new school and think the program changes are also complete. I said many times that the opening of the new building represents only the beginning of the implementation of the proposed program changes. I know people are tired from all the hard work that brought them to this point. However, once the new school is open and underway, we need to rededicate ourselves to the program changes we all agreed to support.

Did the project have a chance given the recent history in the community?

I am grateful I was not told beforehand of recent community history on issues of such importance. I might have concluded that this project could not or would not succeed. I accepted the invitation to be a part of the project, and I never entertained the thought for one second that it would not succeed. So far, my expectations have been met or exceeded. I do not have much to say about this issue, other than to note that I was not alone in holding high expectations for the new high school. Hundreds, if not thousands, of educators, students, and citizens shared this belief.

I am so grateful that the skeptics, doubters, and naysayers never got control of the discourse, or else their low expectations might have affected current reality. The future will show that the students were the ultimate beneficiaries of the high expectations of so many.

What about merging two cultures? Is there going to be trouble ahead?

The existing high schools definitely had school and community cultures that were strong and different. When the staff and students come together at the new school, I am absolutely convinced that there will not be trouble ahead, unless. Unless the adults, both educators and parents, create the expectation that there should and could be trouble. Every time we had joint meetings among staff and students, the climate was positive for the most part. If I may offer an editorial comment, it would be that it is the adults who are beating each other to death at children's events, not the children.

If all the adults in the school and the community approach the new school with high and positive expectations, and move quickly to quell any incidents that might be started by those who enjoy causing trouble, the school population will settle in quickly and without incident.

Will size create alienation and isolation?

The recipe for success that the new high school should follow is to develop and implement systems and strategies at the school so it can be big but behave as if it were small. I believe the action plans that are at various levels of implementation go a long way toward this big but small vision. The first and most obvious example is reflected in the school's houses and thematic programs. Most students and teachers were given their first choice of which house they preferred. This means that, on a daily basis, the student will spend most of his/her time in the same house setting. Each house will have significantly fewer students in its population than did either of the existing schools. This will make it easier for faculty members in each house to get to know their students on a more personal level.

In addition to the house structure, the mission and core values that were embraced focus heavily on the individual student. He/she is the central unit around which the system is organized. The action plans calling for student portfolios will help to maintain emphasis on the individual student as the central focus of the school. Current technology makes it efficient for school systems to focus on groups and individuals at the same time. This reduces the likelihood that individual students will be reduced to a number in a group. For example, technology makes it possible for administrators to have immediate information about how many students are absent on a given day. With a click of the keyboard, they can also learn the names of those who make up that day's list. In addition, information technology makes it cost effective to record a lot of information on students (interests, involvement in activities), as well as their grades. Each of these systemic changes makes it clear that the individual is the central customer of the new high school.

As you can see, I am optimistic about the new high school. I am convinced that the new high school has the potential for realizing the cost effectiveness of a large school (e.g. one library), and at the same time the intimacy we associate with small groups, such as families. I realize that the success of the vision depends on what happens at the beginning of the coming school year.

The members of the joint quality councils and I worried about the size issue. I reassured them that, in his research, management guru Tom Peters found that the key to the success of excellent corporations, such as 3M, was their ability to be both big and functionally small at the same time. I think we have a good plan. The challenge is to execute the plan in the early days following the opening of the new school. If this is done, a culture of caring will take hold. I hope the leadership and the new high school quality council will collect data that will allow them to monitor how well the school does in creating that culture of caring for each and every student.

In the long run what difference might the new school make?

Who can say what difference the new school might make in the future? Those who are skeptical and question the whole effort might argue that it will not make any difference. They see the new school as a journey into excess public expenditure. I am convinced that most of the people who take this position have never been inside either of the two schools that are being replaced.

I am an optimist. I believe the new school is going to change the world! Students will see in the new setting and new programs that the adults in Niagara Falls really value students and education. This knowledge will have a profound effect on the students. The faculty will see new possibilities in the new school and, I'm convinced, will act on those possibilities. The result will be exciting instruction for the students. In addition, the new facility will make it easier for the school district to

Mike Kurilovitch

recruit the best new teachers available. What new teacher would not want to teach in such a beautiful school?

Many northern cities must face redevelopment issues and must find their place in the new economy. The quality of education in a given community plays a significant role in its rebirth. I believe the new Niagara Falls High School will serve a valuable role in future economic development or redevelopment of the city itself. I believe you can not talk about the future of any community without weaving economic development, community development, and educational development together. The new high school serves as a concrete symbol that the people of Niagara Falls are serious about the future of the city.

The school itself has the potential of changing the world! The extent to which the new high school is used as a catalyst for broader community development depends on community leadership. The new school can change the world if the leaders of all the community's institutions want to capitalize on the new high school as a symbol of a new beginning.

I want to thank the Niagara Falls Board of Education for giving me the opportunity to be a part of this ambitious and exciting project. I hope that history will record that the new school altered the future of Niagara Falls for the better. I also hope that history will record that I played at least a small part in its creation.

About the Author:

Mike Kurilovitch is an award-winning journalist and freelance author who has written extensively on the topics of education, justice and social issues. During an eighteen-year career with his hometown *Niagara* (NY) *Gazette*, Kurilovitch was twice honored with the American Bar Association's prestigious Silver Gavel Award for distinguished reporting on the American system of law and justice. He is a two-time winner in the Gannett Co.'s "Best of Gannett" competition, and has also been honored by the New York Newspaper Publishers Association, the New York State Associated Press Association and the New York State Bar Association, among others. Currently a freelance writer for *The Buffalo News*, Kurilovitch, 43, is also involved in the education of elementary aged children. He and wife Teresa have two daughters, Steffany and Meagan.

Printed in the United States
1174800004BA/88-336